Doing Digital

Doing Digital

The Guide to Digital for Non-Technical Leaders

Ved Sen

BEP

BUSINESS EXPERT PRESS

Leader in applied, concise business books

First published in 2022 by
Business Expert Press, LLC
222 East 46th Street, New York, NY 10017
www.businessexpertpress.com

ISBN-13: 978-1-63742-409-4 (paperback)
ISBN-13: 978-1-63742-410-0 (e-book)

Business Expert Press Collaborative Intelligence Collection

First edition: 2022

10 9 8 7 6 5 4 3 2 1

Description

Every business is a technology business, or perhaps it's more accurate to say that every business is a digital business. Whether you work in a large corporation or a small firm, you probably work in a business that's going digital. If anything, the past two years of the pandemic have accelerated our path to digital, with remote work and ecommerce pushing us all into digital modes of working and living. And yet, if you're not a technologist, or if technology and jargon seems opaque to you, you might find it daunting to figure it all out. If you understand business but feel that you don't understand digital and technology well enough, then you're the person I wrote the book for.

If you're a business leader, in a large or small business, you will increasingly find yourself making decisions that need to straddle design, technology, and data, related to your organization, and understand the regulatory aspects of digital trends. You will need to constantly update your view of the world, and use this to refresh your strategy and roadmap more frequently than you've done in the past. This book will help you as well.

Digital means many things to many people. Is it technology? Data? Design? Is it about mobiles? Big data? Agile methods? AI? Often, the answer depends on who you ask, but in reality, it's all of these things. This book will arm you with a conceptual framework with which to understand digital. This will help you understand digital transformation in your business better, but it will also help you make more sense of your next small digital project. It will also give you a simple and robust execution framework (connect, quantify, optimize) to help understand digital cycles.

Along the way, I hope it will demystify a lot of jargon—why APIs are like Lego, or what exponential strategies are about. It is designed to give you a good starting point for your journey in understanding all the many facets of digital. I've written this book to be a jumping-off point for all these topics. This book should give you enough of an understanding and confidence to go looking for more information on the subjects that attract you.

This is not a text book. It's meant to be an easy read. It doesn't assume that you will read the chapters sequentially. Feel free to jump to any topic that's been bothering you.

This is not a book for technologists, it will not dive deep into technology. This is also not a book about digital strategy—there are plenty of good ones out there. This is a guide to digital for non-technical managers, because doing digital is no longer an option. I hope it's fun to read, it's been fun to write.

Keywords

digital; Web; mobile; Web 2.0; Web 3.0; Semantic Web; IoT; XaaS; design thinking; service design; cyber security; containerization; API; voice interfaces; big data; analytics; decision making; knowledge management; data architectures; data science; AI; networks; machine learning; deep learning; ethics; agile; fail fast; sprint; scrum; target operating model; data ethics; graph database; exponential change; discontinuity; networks; disruption; servitization; culture; automation; productivity; robots; connected health; predictive health care; electronic patient records; identity; context; trust; customer experience; future of work; scale-free networks; omnichannel; attention deficiency; transformation; optimization; blockchain

Contents

List of Figures

Disclaimer

All the ideas and frameworks in this book are based on my own observations, and do not necessarily reflect the thinking of my employers, unless specifically called out.

Acknowledgments

My life has been full of fortuitous twists and turns executed with little or no planning. Many of these have led to serendipitous meetings and experiences with amazing people who have changed the course of my thinking with just a conversation. And then there are the many, many friends and family members whose minds I have selfishly explored over many discussions and debates. It is to all these friends, colleagues, and passing acquaintances that I owe a big debt of gratitude for a lifelong evolution of my thinking.

Specifically, I'd like to thank Pradeep Kar for pulling me into the world of technology, and Satish Sukumar who is responsible for some of my earliest conceptual clarity about the Internet and technology.

Kannan R and Shefaly Yogendra deserve their share of blame for this book—it was that conversation of December 2015 that drove me to writing it. Madhu Jalan and Rachel Nolan took time to give me useful feedback, but many, many spared the time to read the book and share their thoughts. Pablo Conde designed the cover. All of you are very special.

To my parents, Kirit and Gopa Sen, and my sister Pragna, who would have been disappointed if I didn't write a book. And to my wife, Karuna Kapoor who takes care of a million things, and inspires me to write.

And to my daughter Maya who is growing up in this digital world and who treats every miracle as mundane.

Introduction

Why This Book?

Everybody has an interpretation of digital business. And much like the blind men and the elephant, we tend to define digital from our perspectives—data enthusiasts will suggest that digital is all about data. Designers will argue that it is in fact about user experience and emotional connects. Technologists of all faiths will put forward their own flavor of digital technology—AI, sensors, or agile development. There are no shortages of catchy acronyms either. SMAC (social, mobile, analytics, cloud) was a very commonly used phrase. Yet, SMAC represents as partial a view as any of the others. I felt that a more complete definition was required, which would embrace all aspects of digital, and yet be short enough to suffice as a definition rather than a description. That was the starting point of my thinking about this book. This led to the creation of a conceptual framework, which hangs off the definition, which I hope will be truly useful for people to deal with the multifaceted nature of digital evolution.

But while a conceptual framework is useful for understanding digital, it may not be as apt in helping people actually do digital projects. We need a simple execution framework to follow from the conceptual one, which can be used while thinking of doing a digital project. This is the connect, quantify, optimize framework, which the title refers to, and what the book drives toward. I hope that the book will therefore help readers to both understand and deliver digital projects, change and transformation in the smallest to the largest projects.

Who Is This Book For?

The book is aimed at the non-technical business user. It does not assume any prior knowledge of technology, software development, or familiarity with any technical jargon. However, it does assume that the reader is engaged in commercial activity already and is exposed to the Web, mobile apps, and has experienced the need to understand digital, whether as a part of a large organization or as an entrepreneur or even a freelancer. No part of this book tries to explain business concepts. It assumes a basic appreciation of the needs of any business, such as competitive strategy, marketing, cost control, and business processes.

While writing the book, I also read and referred to a number of excellent books that are aimed at business leaders and address the challenge of digital strategy. This book is aimed at people who may or may not be in charge of the overall direction and strategy of their businesses. You may be a CEO but you may also be a middle manager or even a junior employee. The point at which a new technology grows exponentially is not when it's invented, but when it undergoes mass adoption. This is true for cars, computers, and mobile phones. Similarly, for a concept such as digital to really take root and grow, we need understanding and adoption by the whole business population, rather than just by business leaders and technologists. In short, this book will not talk about reshaping the directions for your business, but rather will arm you with the understanding to embark on your own digital journey—whether you want to build a mobile app or an ecommerce website, or are trying to digitize the way your department works.

Reading the Book

This is not a textbook. It doesn't follow the structure and format of one, it doesn't set out learning objectives and follow a curriculum. Typical textbooks also often abdicate the responsibility of holding your attention. While there are plenty of conceptual and technical areas to talk through, if on the whole you find the book boring, I would have failed. At the risk of not going deep enough in certain areas, I've tried to pace the book so that it isn't a daunting read.

You are invited to read the book end to end or jump into any section directly. I believe that areas such as AI, networks, and blockchain are some of the areas that are the most forward thinking in this book. But the first section on connect is fundamental.

Every Chapter Can Be a Book

The book takes on a lot of territory as every part of digital is morphing and evolving as we speak. One of the biggest challenges has been to keep the whole book relevant as new events bubble up every week that affect a specific part of the framework. It would be fair to say that every chapter in this book deserves to be a book on its own. So, please treat each chapter as a starting point for further reading for yourself. Feel free to use it as a jumping-off point to then go deeper, do your own research, and flesh out your own model.

A Book, or a Discussion?

In my head, this book, and perhaps every book, is a discussion between the author and the reader. We often have to imagine that conversation, or perhaps every conversation doesn't get completed because of the distance between the writer and the reader. We can address that. Talk to me via twitter (@vedsen/vedcqo@gmail.com) and tell me what you thought. What did you disagree with? What made you nod vigorously? What did you love? Hate? Which parts put you to sleep? What examples do you have that support or challenge what you read here? In the digital world, books should be living documents, and I see this as an ongoing version 2.0 that I'd like to improve with your help and ideas. Talk to me.

PART 1

What Is Digital

CHAPTER 1

Defining Digital

Digital Business: Chasing Rainbows

What Do You Do?

It was a typical evening at a typical networking event. I had just worked my way through some canapés and was sipping my wine appreciatively, when I found myself next to a lady who I recognized from the panel discussion I had just attended. She was a board member at a mid-size company, in the food and beverage business. We exchanged smiles and she said, "What do you do?" "I'm a digital strategy and innovation consultant," I replied. I could see from the arch of her eyebrows that further detail was required. "I help companies with digital strategy and initiatives," I continued.

"But what do you *do*?" she said with a clear emphasis on the last word.

On that occasion, I ended up mumbling something about digital technologies and disruption models, and probably left the lady feeling very confused about what I did. And I remember being angry with myself for a long time after that. This was the classic elevator pitch question, and I fluffed it. Who knows, there could have been a great consulting opportunity at the end of that conversation if it had gone differently. Clearly, I needed to find a better way of expressing what I did.

It also made me reflect on the fact that many clients have had a very different definition of what *digital* means to them. In fact, for many companies that I have known, digital is a sales and marketing issue, or restricted to the customer interface. For others, it's just a technology upgrade. As you can see, an immediate challenge for me was to establish the right definition when talking about digital. A part of the challenge of this answer is the frame of reference of the person asking the question.

To highlight this problem conceptually, let me tell you a funny story about some classmates.

This young couple went house-hunting in Mumbai in the mid-1990s; they were freshly engaged and freshly graduated from business school. He was working for a leading strategy consulting firm; she had just joined a credit rating agency. A prospective landlord asked him the name of his employer, and then said: "so what do they make?" A little taken aback, he explained that they provided strategy consulting and advisory services but didn't actually make anything. It took a few rounds of questioning for the landlord to get his head around this. He then turned to her and asked the same question—"where do you work?" and "what do they make?" At which point, the real estate broker who had been patiently listening to this exchange burst out saying "they make *gajar ka halwa*![1] how does it matter to you?" (*Gajar halwa* is a popular Indian dessert, made with carrots.)

The point is, how much of a jump are you making in your head to understand digital business? For the landlord in my story, the leap from a manufacturing world of *making* to a world of services—of *doing*—was a paradigm shift he struggled to handle. From the time that I started working on web technologies and solutions, I found it very hard to explain to my grandparents exactly what I did. Especially at a time when nobody had Internet at home, so there was no personal experience to draw on.

So ... What Is *Digital*?

As I was saying, despite working in the digital space for years, I was quite stumped when I was asked to define it. Sometimes you can get away with circumlocution (or, to use the technically correct term, waffling!) But given all the hype around digital transformation, I felt that it was a good time to create a working definition. The problem with definitions is the tradeoff between pithiness, abstraction, and comprehensiveness. You can be very pithy but be too abstract, for example, "Digital is the future of business." Or you can take a whole page to define digital, but that's a description and not a definition.

I'm happy to say I'm willing to stick my neck out and try and define digital in less than 25 words. Here's my definition, and I invite you to challenge it, differ with it, or adapt it as you wish. This book uses this definition as a means of structuring the discussion on doing digital.

Digital: exploiting emerging technologies to create customer (user)-centric experiences and data-driven decisions, leading to more agile, competitive, and responsive business models.

(To a nonbusiness person, such as the landlord in my story, a somewhat simpler definition may suffice—using computers to make our lives simpler, and our services and products cheaper and better, but the definition above will work for you as a business person.)

Let's break this up.

Emerging Technologies

Emerging technologies are the driving force of digital. It's the reason why we're having this conversation. But there are many technologies emerging and evolving simultaneously, today.

The frontend: The two big bang events for *digital* was the creation and adoption of the Internet and the launch of the smartphone. The first of these, the Web and its evolving technologies such as HTML5 and JavaScript associated frameworks, continues to evolve to deliver slick websites and applications. Social media is just one of the places we can see this at work. The latter put powerful computers into people's pockets. It democratized access and provided a platform for almost all the other innovations.

The next wave of frontend technologies includes Internet-connected sensors and devices. We are seeing a large-scale adoption of the Internet of things (IOT)—connected and smart objects have the potential to change everything, again, in the way we buy and consume goods and services. The majority of these sensors may have no screens. They may have a voice-driven interface, or they may have no human interface at all—being largely used for machine-to-machine (M2M) communication.

Behind the scenes, a set of technologies that I call *digital infrastructure* is evolving as fast as frontend technologies. Moore's law is being stretched to the limit, but the cost of computing is still heading down, leading to significant improvement in computational capabilities. We are moving our infrastructure to the cloud, creating better means of connecting digital applications to legacy systems, and witnessing the everyday evolution of security-related technologies.

Customer-Centric Interfaces

All this fantastic technology would simply not be usable if it wasn't for design thinking and service design methodologies. Some of this is commonsensical should have been the norm. But the mind-shift is seismic. Industry leading businesses have recognized the need to be customer journey driven. I use the word interface in a broad sense here and not just restricted to screens. The question to ask is "how do your customers, partners, and even employees interface with your business?" Historically, businesses decided how they wanted to run their processes and designed systems and interfaces to match those desired processes. If a bank's preference was for the customer to be in the branch while opening an account, that's how the processes and systems were defined. In the digital world, those interfaces are conceptualized outside-in. This means the starting point is the user. How does the prospective customer want to open the account? What are her constraints? What would make her choice ea/ser and her experience better?

Data-Driven Decisions

Implicitly or explicitly, every decision we make (what to wear to work, for example) is made on the basis of data that we process (what meetings do I have? What is the dress code? What is the weather?). Complex decisions require more sophisticated data. Historically, this data has not been available to us for many large and small decisions. How much to spend on the marketing campaign? Where to open the next store? Who to hire as a program leader for a new business area? How to implement a hot-desking policy? As a consequence, most businesses have relied on *experts* for these decisions, whether they are from within the business or consultants brought in for the purpose. Experts use their wisdom, which is often an implicit accumulation of data from deep experience in that area. What we are witnessing, thanks to digital interfaces and instrumentation, is a collective shift to more explicit data-driven decision making. To do this, we need tools that can store and process gargantuan volumes of data being gathered and processed at ever faster rates. If you've read Michael Lewis's 2003 book *Moneyball*, this is exactly what he speaks about in the context of baseball, and how Billy Beane used data and metrics to assemble a competitive team for Oakland Athletic, despite a modest budget, when everybody else was still working off their experience and instinct.

Competitive and Responsive Business Models

Stripped down to its barebones, a competitive business is simply about serving customers better, faster, cheaper (than your competitors), or some combination of these three. Digital native businesses tend to be better at all three. In part, this is just the benefit of more contemporary tooling. But it's probably more significant that digital businesses are also more responsive. We are used to stability and to treating change as a temporary disruption between periods of stability. Not dissimilar to moving home. Increasingly though, we find ourselves in a state of continuous change. The disruption is not a passing inclemency, but it is the new normal. Think of moving from a house to a caravan, for example. The combination of technologies, design thinking, and data surfeit allows us today to build a responsive and adaptive business model that is able to keep pace with a fast-changing environment. The idea is to not just go get ahead, but stay ahead. Agile methods, and the continuous optimization of businesses and functions, are some of the areas we discuss later in this book.

Connect, Quantify, Optimize

A conceptual understanding of digital is useful, but an execution model is probably more valuable. Connect, quantify, optimize (CQO) is my execution model for digital, and this is why I've structured the book around the CQO model. This model didn't come out of academic research or a moment of epiphany. It came out of dozens of projects and programs with progressive waves of new technologies, out of which the patterns emerged.

In a nutshell, it looks at a cyclical pattern. Good *connections*—that is, digital interfaces such as the Web, mobile, or sensors lead to high-quality, abundant, and granular data. Companies that reshape themselves by putting this data at the heart of their businesses can optimize their entire business for the digital world. You can also optimize a single process or function. The CQO model works at a project level. But you can apply it to the idea of organizational transformation as well.

Eric Ries in his excellent book *The Lean Start Up* refers to a startup business as a *learning machine*. This is because they are able to run this CQO cycle at speed and at scale.

The CQO cycle is virtuous. The more data you get, and the more innovative your optimization cycles, the more powerful your new interfaces and digital connects. Consider the example of Amazon Alexa, and just for the moment, put aside the privacy concerns for the sake of this illustration. Alexa is an almost purely voice-based interface. But thanks to the echo, if you regularly listen to music with a sleep timer often, Amazon knows what time you usually sleep. If you listen to the news in the morning, Amazon knows when you're up. There's a lot of available third-party analysis that can probabilistically deduce things about you from your music choices, including for example your political leanings, your socio-economic status, and your age. Amazon already knows your address and your taste in books and what kind of products you buy online, how many kids you have at home and their ages and genders. In fact, Amazon has a patent for anticipatory shipment.[2] In other words, they ship products to a location near you before you've actually ordered them. It is likely they will travel on Amazon's own planes, and possibly, in future, get delivered to your doorstep or your balcony within 30 minutes of ordering, thanks to Amazon's drones. The point is that Amazon can continue to optimize its business successfully because it's getting the connect and quantify stages right. This is data-driven and industry-shaping digital transformation. For the record, Walmart or Tesco would also know almost as much about you as Amazon does, if you shopped there regularly.

PART 2

Connect

PART 2

CHAPTER 2

The Web—Still Fundamental

The Story of the Web

The European Laboratory for Particle Physics (CERN) was not looking to create the world's biggest techno-social phenomenon, but it was in fact here, in the late 80s that Tim Berners-Lee grappled with an acute problem. Scientific research often involves a large number of references to other works and so as you moved from one paper to the next following a logical link, there was a lot of hunting of the relevant papers involved. Even if you hypothetically put all the relevant research in an electronic format in the same hard drive, it would still take a lot of effort to locate a reference in another paper. Berners-Lee's vision was to create a standard language for linking them physically so you could go straight from one document to a specific part of another, creating what he envisioned as a web of documents. Berners-Lee had already created a hypertext system "Enquire" in 1980, for his personal use.

The mid 80s saw the evolution of the domain name system for naming computers on the Internet—using a domain name server and the now ubiquitous format starting with www and ending with .com. But hypertext models were still proprietary and computer specific. Berners-Lee created a standard protocol—the HyperText Transfer Protocol and an accompanying language—HTML (HyperText Markup Language). Sir Tim-Berners Lee's greatest gift was to open-source HTTP/HTML and for this he will always be remembered the father of the World Wide Web, and the man who gave the digital revolution its first language.

It's just about three decades since the World Wide Web was born, and the first dot.com successes such as Netscape and Mozilla were created. Since then, it's been re-engineered, retooled, turbocharged by broadband, set free by mobile devices, and commercially reinvented more than once. Today, a business website is only noteworthy if it doesn't exist. Websites deliver customers, commerce, and brand messages. But behind the sites themselves, the Web has become the de facto utility on which almost every other digital solution is built. Whether we are watching movies on Netflix or sharing photos on Facebook, storing files on Dropbox or using collaboration tools such as Trello, reading magazines online or banking online, we are using the Web. And whatever you do in the digital world, it's more than likely that the World Wide Web will continue to be a part of your portfolio of interfaces.

Web Technologies Keep Evolving

When you load a web page from an ecommerce website today, a vast array of services and systems are at play behind the screen. The simple HTML page envisioned by Berners Lee has long been replaced by a combination of programmatically generated commercial data and content. Extensible Markup Language (XML) enabled more versatile web pages, while Cascading Style Sheets (CSS) dramatically improved the formatting and control over layout. HTML5, the most recent evolution of the original HTML standard, absorbs a lot of the capabilities of XML and CSS, and also enables much better use of multimedia content.

As browsers have matured and evolved, they can access more computing power and memory. The amount of logic that can be handled within the browser has also increased. JavaScript in many flavors is now almost universally used for the front-end development of Web applications. But the complexity of individual web pages is also much higher. The use of Asynchronous JavaScript And XML (AJAX) allows individual bits of pages to be refreshed without refreshing the whole page. You may have seen picture galleries or conditional forms that refresh subsequent fields based on choices made, again without reloading the full page. Additionally, jQuery is increasingly used for generating more interactive and rich front-end interfaces.

This collection of Web technologies and development tools defined broadly by browser-based access and Web architectures is also critical to the way companies are increasingly running internal processes and functions. Web architectures are by design loosely coupled, so they allow for ongoing evolution and running repairs and upgrades. Original Web architectures used a natural separation of front end (interface and experience) and back end (data and processing, broadly speaking). You may have come across terms like MEAN stack (Mongo, Express, Angular, and Node) or the LAMP stack (Linux, Apache, MySQL, and PHP/Python). Both of these are essentially combinations of coding, database, and design frameworks. Both are *open source* and have millions of technologists and supporters who all believe in the principle of sharing. As a result, these technologies continue to be free but have evolved very quickly into highly robust toolkits.

Websites are now responsive by design. Thanks to the proliferation of mobile phone and tablet models with a range of form factors, websites need to be ready for any size of screens and still perform adequately—which means that the design and content need to be elegant and with very little loss of experience. A responsive website will mold itself to any device and will intelligently reorganize content to ensure that it is always readable. An adaptive website is similar but will work toward a few predefined sizes.

The Business of the Web

Most of us recognize the Web today as a confluence of communication channels and virtual marketplaces. It has become the de facto way of conducting business for many organizations and a preferred way of shopping by millions of customers worldwide, with the browser as its primary interface. Yet, the Web is still evolving, and it's worth taking note of some of the more recent evolutionary steps that the Web and browsers have taken.

Workspaces, Not Windows

Thanks to the increased bandwidth and computing power available within the browser, multimedia content and interactive content, and video, have all become commonplace, within the browser. The browser has been described as the "operating system of the Internet." This is especially vivid when you think about using tools such as *Google Docs*, which allow you to run the entire office productivity suite inside a browser with no installed software. Rather than being just a tool for viewing web pages, the browser is in fact now a workspace that integrates you to the Web. Google Chrome is by a margin the most popular browser today, and it comes with a lot of extensible options—buttons and links you can add to make regular tasks easier—from bookmarking content or blocking ads. The browser is a critical productivity environment if used correctly. Tools like Evernote, which has 25 million users, can work almost within the browser as well as via a desktop application.

> Tip: As far as possible, a version of your service should be available to access and consume from a browser.

Monopolies, Not Perfect Competition

The Web has played its role in blurring national borders. Goods and services flow freely across the world today even at a consumer level, because of the democratic access to the Internet and low barriers of entry. This is why, a businesswoman sitting in Spain can hire a college graduate in Singapore via a platform built and owned by an American company to do online research on price comparisons. This irreverence for borders has played a big role in creating a single global market mentality in many categories. Some would argue that this democracy of information and low cost of entry creates a good approximation of perfect competition. Yet ironically, the Web has created a monopolistic model because in this single global market with free flow of information, why would anybody go to the second-best option? Bear in mind that China apart, we now effectively have a dominant global search engine, a dominant global social network, and a globally dominant ecommerce provider. The idea of a long tail as a commercial model may be replaced by a very long tail as a meagre sustainment of an esoteric fringe. I believe that regulation permitting, it is likely that high street banking, or retail utilities could all end up with similar market structures with one or two players dominating a market.

Tim Wu in his book *The Master Switch*[1] talks about the recurrent pattern where every new communications technology—such as the telegraph or the Internet, starts out with the promise of a brave new world of democratizing content but ends up with a monopolistic model.

> Tip: In a digital industry, you need to be among the top two players in your market.

Gray, Deep, and Dark

We've come to think about the Web as an open and searchable environment, but it's worth keeping in mind that overwhelmingly large parts of the Web are not visible to us. There are plenty of sites that opt out of search engines and block crawlers. This is often referred to as the deep web. Recent regulations in Europe around the right to be forgotten have created another gray area about what can and will be found on search engines. The deep web accounts for 90 percent of the Web, with the visible or *surface web* that we all use regularly just form 10 percent. The deep web includes mostly techno-legal content and systems that just don't want to be accessed by the average public user. This would include database servers that serve ecommerce websites, and government-sensitive content for example. Then there's the dark web. This is specifically a part of the deep web that is designed for anonymity and managed through special (Tor) servers and clients. This is the part of the Web that is extremely secretive by choice and is used therefore both for activists who value privacy above all and for nefarious purposes beyond the reach of the law. It is highly unlikely that your business model needs to consider the dark net, unless you work in law enforcement, espionage, crime, or quasi legal areas. Or perhaps on the engineering of the dark net itself. But it's worthwhile recognizing the deep and gray areas of the Internet, at the very least, from a security perspective.

The Digital Supermarket

The Web is also evolving as we speak. More sensors are being connected to the Web, and more data will be openly available for merging with your own and creating new meaning. In this sense, the Web is a giant digital supermarket. Because it's not just data, but services and functionalities, which you can consume or combine with tools, that are all available off the Web. You can visit a survey tool, a video streaming site, or a calendar online. But you can also create a single page using these individual functionalities by simply letting these services connect through your page. This makes the Web a giant box of components. I would argue that a lot of organizations need to curtail their natural response to develop new functionality and write new code. Instead, the first step should be to see how far you can get by assembling existing bits of functionality and code, and once you have an initial prototype or beta version, you can then explore the option of rewriting key missing bits or those areas that are critical to your service and can be improved upon.

> Tip: Always start by exploring what you can pick and combine from existing services, rather than write new code.

Awaiting Web 3.0

All that happened between the initial dial-up Internet and restrictive browser experience, and today's broadband-friendly rich media websites, as I've described is roughly known as Web 2.0. A simple way of classifying the stages of the Web is as follows: 1.0 was the read-only Web. 2.0 was all about read, write, and operate. So, what will Web 3.0 bring?

A number of technologies are staking claim to be the definitive basis for Web 3.0. Tim Berners Lee started the discussion around the semantic web, which understands context. For example, when you search for Vertigo, are you searching for the condition or the film? Or when you're looking for a restaurant called Chinatown, are you able to get past the film reviews and the street maps in your city? This is intrinsically connected with how your data is stored and used. Sir Tim's current venture is called Solid and deals with this problem. Web 3.0 is also going to be driven via the IOT wave, so an order of magnitude more connections will be made. Your car, or your oven, or your mattress may all be endpoints for Web 3.0. This is the vision of IOT as we know it. In recent times, it feels like the Blockchain and Crypto community will dominate the Web

3.0 discourse. If they are right, Web 3.0 will be distributed, secure, and transaction-driven, with a closer approximation to the immersive cyber-space concept envisioned by William Gibson.[2] This table is a useful way to understand the past and future of the Web.

	Web 1.0	Web 2.0	Web 3.0
Access	Dial-up	Broadband, mobile 3G/4G	Mobile 5G
Speeds	Kilobytes	Megabytes	Gigabytes
User focus	Read only	Read/write/create	Read/write/create/own/ trust
Devices	Desktop computers/ laptops	Mobile devices	IOT sensors/automobiles/ health care devices, etc.
Number of end Points	Millions	Billions	Trillions
Dominant Use	Publish, read, e-mail	Collaborate, create, ecommerce, stream	Decentralized finance, identity systems, autono-mous systems

Figure 2.1 Web 1.0, 2.0, and 3.0, an overview

CHAPTER 3

The Social Interface—Media and Marketplace

In 2004, when Mark Zuckerberg was still figuring out how to make Facebook work at Harvard, a 24-year-old woman in Sunderland, England, was struggling financially after losing her old economy job. Ironically, it was in a print factory, and it was the only job she had ever had. She had a £400 rent to pay and no idea how to get it. In desperation, she spent £15 on the Avon program and started to sell Avon's cosmetic products to her friends and family as well as door to door. She was amazed to find that she sold over £18,000 worth of cosmetics in a few weeks—which by Avon's 20% commission model, would have earned her over £3,600. She and her husband decided to build their own network of sales people and work together full time on this model. In 2010, Debbie Davis was recognized as Britain's first Avon millionaire, with a network of 2,500 people working with her.

The Avon Ladies were a brand unto themselves, and they sharpened a model that Tupperware had pioneered in the 1940s and 1950s. But both depended on a couple of common principles—direct sales and social networks. Not the online kind, but good old social connections. People whom you would trust, and do dinner parties with. Business has always relied on social connections, so we shouldn't be surprised that the online social networks of today are so valuable to businesses.

Facebook has outlasted a host of other social networks such as MySpace, Tribe, Bebo, Orkut, and so on to reach 2.89 billion worldwide active users as of mid-2021, which means nearly 40 percent of the world's population now uses Facebook regularly. (WhatsApp, owned by Facebook has another 2.5 billion.) So it is understandable that when we say social, we imply Facebook. Twitter has under 200 million users, and LinkedIn has about 600 million, for comparison. In recent times, TikTok has grown spectacularly, reaching a billion users and is a preferred social network for many, especially younger people who tend to eschew Facebook, so this is one to watch.

The Value of Social Networks

You probably know that listening to consumers is one of the biggest benefits from social media—whether replying to direct messages or analyzing sentiments. But here are a few other ways social media adds value.

Mass-Customized, Micro-Targeted

Facebook and other major social networks are effectively today's mass media. There are ever fewer opportunities to address very large audiences, with the fragmentation of traditional media. But also, because no other platform as much intimate access to people's lives as Facebook does, it's also mass customizable. Where else can you direct a marketing message that will be received by divorced, democrat-supporting Americans with an interest in heavy metal and tattoos, living in Ohio?

Sentiment analysis is now a common term in business. In 2010, a couple of MIT scientists showed that tracking Twitter mentions provided a more accurate forecast for the success or failure of a film than the best alternatives of the time, such as the Hollywood Stock Exchange, which was by itself a kind of social sentiment aggregation platform. The writer and Entrepreneur Christian Rudder says that we are seeing the death of traditional market research—because we no longer have to ask people questions when between Google, Facebook, and other platforms we can see the actual choices, views, and opinions of people at a larger scale, and without the sampling bias.[1] Data from the major platforms is deeper and wider than any market research can match. Moreover, it is naturally a longitudinal study because it retains data about people—so over the next

20 years and beyond, social networks will be able to track the evolution of thinking for an entire generation and more.

Influence as a Service

This means a switch from traditional advertising—which is all about having the loudest voice and saying the funniest things, to a model where you have the most number of others rooting for you. The big opportunity here is to convert your customers into brand ambassadors. And you know which sounds more authentic. The recent rise of *influencers* is an additional factor in this mix. Ryan Kaji, who lives in Texas and is about 10 years old, earned close to $30m for his YouTube videos in 2019, largely involving unboxing toys and educational material. This feels a little bit like we've come full circle back to celebrity endorsements on television in the 1980s, doesn't it?

Trust as a Service

The link between commercial and social networks is as old as civilization, and this is finding new expression today. Facebook has dabbled in commerce, shopping, and payments via FB messenger and WhatsApp. The most recent being the efforts to create a cryptocurrency called Diem (earlier known as Libra). Payments are also now available via Facebook messenger, in the United States. In China, WeChat has long since integrated payments into its messaging solution. Professional networks such as LinkedIn have evolved into a leading hiring platform. TripAdvisor also allows you to book hotels and restaurants through its portal. New banks such as Revolut and Monzo also allow you to easily pay contacts. Open banking regulations have also made it much easier to set up payment and transaction services. The backbone of commerce is trust, and that's what social networks provide. Services such as Trustpilot have actually created commercial models by providing *trust as a service* for these community sites. And large number of services allow you to sign up with your Google or Facebook credentials. This is another way in which social networks are providing identity and authentication, to enable trust. eBay was an early mover in this space, as they rolled out a rating system that has become a sine qua non of almost every ecommerce or transactional site.

Exploiting Social Networks

The Challenge of Transparency

The era of pervasive social networking also brings challenges for businesses. Most notably, it marks an end to the time where companies could mask average products with great advertising and marketing. Bad news travels fast on the network, and the implication of this is that companies need to go back to the drawing board and ensure that products are up to the mark, or they will be found out very quickly. Inefficient airline operations, poor technical support for electronics, or bad assembly for a flat packed item of furniture—all of these get noticed and shared quickly. The first stop for surviving in the connected world is to ensure product and service quality. You can then follow through by providing information, building trust and transparency, and finally move on to socialization. This is why, TripAdvisor is often a first stop for holiday planners, or reading the reviews is essential part of shopping on Amazon.

Measuring Social Value

You could say that social media is also a cesspool of entrenched opinion, conspiracy theories, and trolls. And you'd probably be right as well. There's a lot that social media businesses need to do, to address these concerns. But even within this environment, it offers brands a chance to identify what they stand for. Nike's deal with Colin Kaepernick is a good example of this. In 2019, Nike agreed to a Kaepernick request to recall a shoe with an objectionable symbol on it. Nike's stock went up by 2 percent on the back of this, amounting to a gain of more than $2.5 billion. Social media connects people to issues, and allows us to quantify the value of those connections, irrespective of which side of various political debates you're on.

The Value of Connect

This used to be the mobile firm Nokia's tagline. In the context of this book, we need to see the value of social media as the primary way that people connect with each other in the 21st century. If human history has been driven by how we connect, then the early marketplaces on the banks of rivers, and the pubs and coffee houses of the industrial era, have given way to the online melting pot of social media. Many banks now use social media as an analysis tool for evaluating risk profiles of individuals.

Tip: The real gold dust in social media is creating a currency of trust.

CHAPTER 4

Mobile—The Remote Control for Your World

Asos, the online apparel business, sells more on mobile devices than on desktop websites, and gets almost 70 percent traffic on mobile websites. As much or more ecommerce gets transacted on mobile devices than on desktops today. Many billion-dollar companies such as Snap, Spotify, and Uber work primarily on mobile devices. By some estimates, more people own a mobile phone across the world, than toothbrushes.

The smartphone device evolution has plateaued. Since the passing of Steve Jobs, there hasn't been a slew of new and significant improvements in the device itself. The immediate future looks rich for battery technology and folding screens. In the past 12 to 18 months, even if you bought the latest iPhone or a top-of-the-line android phone, you're not likely to find dramatically new features in there—more like marginal improvements in screens, batteries, cameras, and sensors. This has made developing mobile apps and solutions easier as variety of phones in the wild has reduced. This is a good example of why the actual transformative impact of new technology tends to play out over a much longer period through mass adoption as the world starts to figure out how best to exploit the new technology.

The Smartphone: Four Important Perspectives

Whether your users are consumers, business-to-business (B2B) customers, or employees, it is likely that they have a smartphone, and that they depend on it for a lot of things.

The Everything Device

Perhaps it's an injustice to call the smartphone a phone. They are pocket-sized computers capable of doing many things, of which one is making phone calls. Today, my smartphone is my Internet browser, bank branch, e-mail client, note taker, airline check-in desk, the gateway to my social life, my music player, calendar, camera, task manager, watch, and newspaper. It's also my TV remote, my parking assistant, tube map, wallet, game console, television program recorder, and fitness assistant.

Pocket Rocket

You may have heard the comparison that people often make—the iPhone has more computing power than Apollo 11, which took Neil Armstrong and others to the moon. To make this a more vivid comparison, the iPhone 6 has 130,000 more transistors, has a clock frequency that is 32,000 times faster, and can process about 80 million times the number of instructions per second, compared with the Apollo Guidance Computer (AGC) used in Apollo 11. No doubt the AGC was advantaged by not having to also deal with thousands of photographs, videos, and WhatsApp messages alongside performing its primary role!

Deeply Personal

We also know now that smartphones are intensely personal devices. Looking at somebody else's phone is probably even more intrusive than looking through their purse or handbag. Most spouses and couples would not look through each other's phones out of respect for privacy. From the moment that you start using a new phone, you start to customize it to your needs. Consider the smartphones of any two people—their preferences and indeed their personalities are distinctly mapped through their choice of applications, and the way they are arranged. If you're on your third or fourth smartphone, you probably have a very set way of organizing your icons, which is the first thing you do with a new phone. People notice their phone is missing long before they notice if their wallet is missing. This identity extension and always-on device allows us to engage in real time with any product, service, or brand we choose, and conversely, it gives any trusted provider the chance to reach us in real time with our permission, in a 24 × 7 manner.

Remote Control for the World

The smartphone is effectively our *remote control for the world*. I can control my lights, my music, my television set top box, and my home heating. I can also interact with my daily bus, train or tube, taxi, and my professional and personal network. The idea of control is a very powerful one. Even though we're not necessarily controlling the world, we are definitely empowering ourselves. I don't control the speed of the bus, but thanks to my smartphone, I can compare alternative routes and make the best decision about whether to wait for the bus, or take the tube or follow some other route to my destination. I decide when I want to bank and how I want to interact with my providers, because I can do it anywhere and anytime. The smartphone has been the biggest contributor to the transfer of control and power to the customer, in the way service providers deal with them. While customer centricity was always a principle for businesses, the smartphone made it tangible.

Four Ways the Smartphone Usage Is Evolving

Augmented Reality

One of the most hyped aspects of mobile solutions was the promise of augmented reality (AR). As with most technologies, it went through what the analyst firm Gartner aptly call the hype curve. Initial overexpectation about what is possible is followed by crushing disappointment as the technology is too nascent to deliver all the things it's supposed to. After which it often grows slowly at a steady and natural pace, through to adoption. AR seems to have been through this hype and disappointment more than once. The idea is that you look at an object through your phone camera, and it will recognize the object and overlay additional information on it. It could be a publicly accessible building—say a house for sale on a high street, which shows you the details of the house. It could also be a private and specific application. Educational apps use these, so you can point your phone at a picture of a dinosaur in a text book, and see the animal in 3D along with more details about its diet. Or it can be purely imaginary, such as the Pokémon game, which went viral in 2016. All of these are real examples. Starting in 2017, both Android and iOS devices have AR engines baked into the operating system (OS), so the load of building AR tools is even lower. I expect more AR applications to be commonplace soon.

Mobile Identity and Payments

Mobile devices are used for identity and authentication over the world. In the developing world, any online service you use, from car hire, to ordering food, or accessing your bank account, will involve a one-time password (OTP) sent to your mobile device. Banks and businesses now use app features to generate passcodes that need to be re-entered into the website. The principle in both cases is the same—the security model combines something only you know (your password) with something only you have (your mobile phone). Additional encryption, biometrics, and even location information are used for additional layers of security.

Mobile Passport and Wallet

You've probably had experiences of airplane boarding cards, or train tickets being saved as *virtual passes* in your mobile wallet. We aren't yet at a stage where mobile devices can be virtual passports and identity cards. But the idea that your mobile phone should be an extension of your core identity system makes a lot of sense, given its additional geo-location and the kind of biometric information it already captures (face recognition, fingerprints, etc.). The problem isn't technology, it's working out the interaction between multiple ecosystems, and working out the data privacy, and ethical problems in sharing this data.

Presence

This is an interesting premise. In the pandemic, mobile devices were used by a number of countries for track and trace. Something that also brought

Apple and Google developers together. Your mobile device is a marker of your presence or a locator for those to whom you provide permission. I frequently use this feature to track my daughter as she returns from school so I can be at the bus stop just a few minutes before she arrives. How else could we use the value of presence? Every time that a customer logs into your website, you know they're there. You see everything they click on and do. What would it be like if we could do the same in the real world? A retail store doesn't know who's in the store till they come to the till. Whereas, a website can not only see who is on the site, they can customize the offers they make to the shoppers, and provide special treatment and experience to their best customers. But a retailer could, if customers were incentivized to declare their presence in the store. Then you could make special offers based on their shopping history, and even give the best customers a fast-track checkout, like a business-class experience.

Tip: Think of the ways to help people manage their identity, optimize their time, transact with their ecosystem, and interact with their environment.

Serving the Mobile User

The Mobile Website

There are almost 6.5 billion smartphones in the world today. About 80 percent people in the United States, the UK, France, and Germany have smartphones as we get into the 2020s. It's far more likely that more people are accessing your website via mobile than via a desktop or laptop computer. To underscore the obvious, the mobile user's requirements and priorities are often different from the desktop users', so this is more than just a shrinking of the Web interface.

Mobile App or Mobile Website?

Mobile apps don't really compete with mobile websites. Apps are typically for those people who are declaring an interest in deepening a relationship with your brand or product. Given a choice, people download apps so that they can access a service more easily, or because it gives them a better quality of experience. Either way, they make the investment of time, to download and use your app, presumably because they are regular users of the service. I would not download the mobile app for every airport I visited, but because I typically use the Heathrow airport many times a year, and sometimes more than once a month, I would absolutely use the app to make my travel easier. Imagine a scenario where your best customers or users self-select and make themselves visible and accessible to you. This is what a mobile app can do, for the business. Consequently, the requirements from a mobile app may be completely different from that of a mobile website. You need the app if you want to build a deeper relationship with your top 20 percent customers, or those customers looking for a deeper relationship with you. Most businesses need the desktop website, the mobile website, and the app. They actually serve three very different kinds of needs and markets.

Mobile First or Mobile Only?

You may have come across the term *mobile first*—this refers to the trend of businesses to build their mobile sites and apps before they build their desktop websites. This is a nod to the primacy of mobile. But I believe that it will go further, into a category of mobile only solutions. As highlighted in the opening paragraph before, Snapchat and Spotify (and WhatsApp and Uber!) are effectively mobile only businesses. And with year on year, the decline in the personal computer (PC) market, we are witnessing the switch from PCs to tablets and phones for households. This means there are some segments of your market with people who won't have a desktop PC at all, and will expect to transact with you via a mobile device only, or a laptop or tablet at best. Are you ready for the mobile only customer? Is your business or product set up for an end-to-end life cycle of consumer engagement on a mobile device?

Developing Mobile Apps—What's the Right Model Today?

Language

The right answer to "what language should you build your mobile apps in?" seems to change every year. Last year, the answer was React. This year, you see a lot of debates between Flutter and React. Fortunately, the implication of this decision has also become much simpler to manage. There was a time when the pace of change of the device demanded new versions of the app for android and iOS devices, and you had to go the extra mile to utilize all the benefits of the device. Now any app developed on React, for example, largely works well across most of the major devices. You may still need to worry about the unique capabilities of some devices and test for their unusual form factor—for example for the folding screen of a new Samsung phone. But over the past few years, entire categories of cross-platform mobile development tools have come and gone. If you tried building apps over the last 10 years, you may remember companies like Antenna, Appcelerator, Cyclo, Kinvey, Kony, and many others. All of which have been acquired and integrated into larger software companies. That in itself tells the story of the evolution of mobile development—it's become a lot more standardized. It's a reminder that the debates around mobile development were not as religious as they appeared, say five years ago.

Tip: Be prepared for this answer to change every 3 to 4 years or even faster.

Native Versus Web Apps

The other debate that has raged in the past was around native versus Web applications. Web applications allowed the same code to be run on the Web and mobile phones, or within a native *shell*. HTML5 has enabled rich features for Web apps. Today, all of these strands have converged, thanks to tools such as *React Native*, a development framework created by Facebook. These allow the use of versions of JavaScript for programming, but they in turn generate native iOS and Android apps. Apps are now much more lightweight and rely on getting data from the backend via APIs. Although there are purists who may have strong preferences for what development platform to use, this is probably not a debate you want to get into, in the 2020s.

Device Versus Network

A useful way to look at this is also to think about the triangle of device, network, and application. For the first few years of the smartphones, the devices were more powerful than the network could handle. It made sense therefore to put more of the processing on the device, and only use the network to send data back and forth. This led to heavier apps, and a preference for native applications as well. Over the past five years, with the availability of 4G and ubiquitous Wi-Fi, bandwidth has ceased to be a constraint. Today, apps can be much more lightweight, and instead get both the data and executables off the Web, for example to run within a browser. This is not different from the way desktop applications have been replicated by the in-browser experience for office applications like presentations, Word processing, and spreadsheets.

> Tip: Your best customers will identify themselves by downloading your app. Treat them well.

Wireframing

A number of tools have been popular for wireframing over the years, but three stand out for me—Balsamiq, Invision, and Axure. Other options include InDesign, Adobe, and Sketch. Building a prototype or wireframe yourself is an excellent way to experience first-hand the flow you are going to put your users through, and you may find it helps to iron out a lot of the wrinkles in the smooth functioning of the app and the process.

Low-Code/No-Code

An entirely new category of tools has emerged for enterprise apps, which are particularly good for deploying simple apps within your business, that won't justify the effort of a consumer grade application development. Let's say you want to build a sales app for a new product to support your global sales team—so you have a hundred or so users, and a simple structure. Low-code/no-code (LCNC) tools allow you to build these apps using standard templates, and even connect to your enterprise applications. Microsoft Power Apps and Mendix are two names that seem to have gained traction in recent times.

Enterprise Apps

Mobile apps are still under-exploited in the enterprise. Especially with the advent of LCNC tools as we've just discussed. Almost every employee facing process the Web and paper interfaces to corporate processes and services—expenses, travel statements, approval workflows, forms, and feedback—all of these should already be app-enabled for quicker and easier access and workflows. As executives and managers face the challenge of productivity and time paucity while dealing with hot-desking and more distributed work environments, they need to be able to quickly and efficiently perform basic tasks in a way that has been designed to make it seamless and easy. Expense statements are often black holes in large organizations. And yet, there are plenty of existing solutions from companies Expensify who can dramatically reduce this pain. You can scan a bill, and with available technology, it can recognize the category of expenses, date, location, and amounts. The system can do most of the work involved with classifying and submitting the expense and just present you with a approve/edit option. It can also encourage people to submitting expenses as they happen rather than after six months, which allows the business to be more current in terms of managing and monitoring expenses. In a world where creating such an app wouldn't even require you to write a lot of code, it seems like a shame.

Enterprise mobility usually requires a device management or mobile application management solution through which your corporate e-mails and other access is enabled. This allows the business to separate personal from corporate information on the phone, and if required, wipe all the data from the corporate container without impacting personal information. It also allows the firm to manage the versions, access and usage of enterprise apps, and execute policies. These policies could even include geo-fencing or allowing a feature to be used only within a specific geographical location, or the opposite. For example, it could disable your camera within a certain radius of a high-security environment.

Tip: Enterprise mobile apps are an under-explored minefield of opportunity for productivity and value.

Summary

We are at this curious point in the story of mobile apps—where they hype has gone, but the real transformation is very much in play. The impact of mobiles in organizations will only grow over the next few years, and I definitely expect smartphones to be a primary interface for most consumers and office workers for increasing proportions of their personal and professional needs.

CHAPTER 5

The Internet of Things

Understanding the IOT

The tech industry is often guilty of pushing technology solutions to consumers without focusing on the benefits, the emotions and simplicity. The IOT, on the other hand, is a pithy catchphrase, but by itself, it means very little when it comes to actually buying, implementing, or solving something. The IOT is a neologism coined by Kevin Ashton[1] to encapsulate a number of related concepts. It involves smart and connected products, multiple types of open and closed networks, robotics, cloud-based access, decision analytics, and functions ranging from monitoring to control and optimization. Many people also refer to M2M communications, which are distinct from the content and functionality that is designed for consumption by people, or even people interacting with machines.

At its heart, it involves allowing everyday objects or *things* to be connected to the Internet via sensors and accessible via the Internet. These could be pipes managed by utility companies or buoys in the ocean, but are increasingly consumer-grade devices as well. The sensors themselves are also varied—based on what it is that they are sensing. Pressure sensors on a utility pipe could help ensure smooth water flows, or track leaks, whereas motion sensors on buoys can provide early warnings of tsunamis. The data from these sensors may be public or private but can be married with other data to drive outcomes for users. The data may also be read by systems to automate decisions based on preset limits. For example, if the buoys show that the waves are dangerously high, the system can send out a message to vessels in the area.

The IOT therefore includes communication between machines, between people and machines, and also between people and people via machines. It includes wearables, and all manners of sensors, and an ever-increasing ocean of data, and an implicit assumption of an economically viable, reliable, and available network.

Microelectromechanical sensors (MEMS), which are smaller than a millimeter in size, are a very popular type of sensor. They go into a lot of consumer products—including smartphones and inkjet printers. They are also found in health care devices, such as stents. The launch of the iPhone created a spike in demand of 10 million MEMS in 2007, but the MEMS market grew to 15 billion in 2015! You can almost pick any number for the global sensor market in five years, and it might turn out to be a conservative estimate. One estimate quotes 100 billion sensors by 2025, with a revenue of $10 trillion. You're probably already using more sensors that you know, and you're definitely consuming data from more sensors than you think.

Michael Porter and James Heppelman in their very lucid HBR article posit[2] that all products in future should have mechanical/electrical components, but also software components and communication components. These three collectively make products smarter and ultimately evolve to product systems (e.g., home security) and then to a *system of systems* model (e.g., connected homes)—which spans an entire problem domain, according to the authors. The kind of activities that we can perform on smart products evolves from monitoring, to control, optimization, and then to autonomy. Ultimately, this leads to improved competitive performance via operational efficiencies and strategic positioning choices. Often, forcing the question "what business are we in?"

> Tip: Consider the number of sensors that are at play in your smartphone, as you use it.

Internet of *Your* Things

Try this exercise. List all the *things* you interact with. From your house and home to the trains you take and from the clothes you wear to the hotel room you might live in on my work trip or holiday. You'll quickly realize that the list is too long to actually complete. But also, you might see that this is a hierarchical list. Your home, for example, is a complex construct, and comprises many sub-things. For example, rooms, walls, plumbing. Some of these, such as *heating* may have further subcomponents—radiators, boilers, and so on. You can then try and imagine how you would want each of these things to behave to make your life easier. I would like my wardrobe to be aware of my calendar and the weather and recommend to me choices for what to wear with visual combinations of clothes to wear every morning. You might want your coffee machine to sense when you're up and about and start brewing your favorite cup of coffee, and remind you when it's ready.

Let's consider just one of these things—windows. Everybody has windows at home, and they affect our everyday lives. They have states (open/shut), based on the environment and conditions. We typically associate safety, air conditioning, and sunlight with windows being open or closed, based on the weather, time of day, and so on. You can construct a table in your mind with benefits and the associate state or activity for those benefits, and the conditions under which they need to be activated. For example, when it rains, your windows need to be closed so that your house can be dry. During a pleasant and clear day with lots of sunshine, your windows need to be open so that your house can be aired. At night, they need to be closed so that you can be safe. Perhaps they can change their level of transparency in response to the amount of sunlight.

You would be right in thinking that all that we've described above can happen with smart windows, which need not be connected to the Internet. We need to distinguish between smart (computation capability) and connected (communication capability), and not treat them as synonyms. Some windows come with a remote control, they can be opened and closed, and they can also react to weather conditions and close if left open when it starts to rain. They are actually smart, in some way, and possess limited capability to communicate. They're just not on the Internet. The challenge of this model is that your ability to control these outcomes is limited to the preset automations and your being in close proximity—that is at home, and with the right remote.

Some of my home windows have rain sensors, which allow them to automatically close if it starts to rain, but they don't have a sun sensor, which allows them to reopen when the sun comes out again. Actually, for all my windows, I would like a certain level of intelligence. I'd like to be reminded if ground floor windows are left open at night or when I'm away. If I had pollen allergies, I would probably like to be alerted if the pollen count is too high, or have the windows close. I would like to be able to open all multiple windows or close them, even if I'm not at home, based on weather conditions. I might even have settings for *sunny day*, which applies a set of commands to all windows. This is the optimization that we ultimately want to get to. These controls should extend to blinds because they are a part of my window product systems, whereas currently, we might have completely different suppliers for these two products (windows and curtains/blinds). Any maker of smart windows must therefore consider blinds and curtains as a part of their product system.

Now, considering any smart and connected product, we could argue that they have sensors, which generate data, which are used by apps, which enable access and control of the product, and provide additional functions that ultimately deliver a benefit. The sensors are obviously on-board the device/product. But the data generated could be anywhere, typically on a cloud, so that the apps and the access can take place through any connected control point (such as a mobile phone).

This is where the IOT really kicks in. In my window example, for the *Velux* models that we have installed, the data, access, applications, and controls all sit within a closed system involving the window and the remote control. A mature IOT model requires a cloud-based data and access model and an ability to use the data and control/monitor the product from any device and application that is authorized. So, I could then control the windows from office if I wanted to air the living room on a sunny day.

Tip: Think about how you would like things to behave if you could make them follow some logical rules.

The Network of Your Things

Many smart products today are capable of performing advanced functions autonomously, which have nothing to do with the Internet of anything.

The Roomba smart vacuum cleaner is a great example of an exceptional product that doesn't really need to connect to the Internet for its everyday operation of intelligent vacuuming.

Most individual products also tend to ignore or be indifferent to the network effect, which kicks in when we consider multiple elements in the same network. My windows may be rain-sensitive, but I might have other devices, products, and appliances at home, which may be influenced by the occurrence of rain. Does each product need to have its own rain sensor? In my IOT wish list, my smart windows can communicate to other appliances at home. The washing machine can run an extra spin cycle when it rains, so clothes dry in the same time, and conversely, when it's sunny, it can reduce the spin cycle to conserve energy. This is when we get to the real IOT. Today, the way we connect devices is actually via the cloud. Each device connects to its cloud and data is shared across providers at the backend.

> Tip: Think about how devices could share functionality or information across an environment—such as a home or factory.

B2B and M2M

A significant part of the IOT will continue to involve machines talking to machines behind the scenes in ways that will not involve humans at all. This may well be the lion's share of the IOT in the years to come. This could be cars, trains, buses, and transport infrastructure communicating with each other, or your devices sending data back to manufacturers systems, or even production systems and factory infrastructure exchanging information—all of which will be used for decision making that will go on without us as humans being explicitly involved. A simple example that has been discussed often of late is you run your dishwasher at night after dinner, but your smart dishwasher *talks* to your smart meter and runs the cycle after midnight, when the energy cost is at its lowest. The communication, data exchange, and decision making are all happening without your explicit involvement.

Challenges

I've made the point more than once about how easy the browser-based Web world was. In the IOT world, though, we have to think about the hardware, the embedded system, the interface and communication protocol, the environment, and purpose—almost everything has to be designed from scratch. What's the user interface of a *thing*? If it's a sensor in a coffee machine versus in a door, how should we access the data, how can interact with the thing? The design challenge moves from the *interface* design to experience and even environment design, and it will vary from fitting an antenna while managing heat dissipation, to figuring out how to retain product aesthetics and usability while adding sensors to running shoes. Service design, which we discuss later, is fundamental to the creation of IOT models. We must take a design centric view and build from there. That's the only way we'll get around to focusing on the right problems to solve, to ensure adoption.

Ultimately, this will create and shift value, destroy old models, and create entirely new services. We usually find it easier to think of things that will be better, rather than different. A common example of better, is that a future fridge will tell us when it's out of milk, or order it on our behalf. The fridge is still doing the same basic job. An example of different might be that our fridge will become a health care device and do an analysis of all the food we've consumed over a month, and give us a health trend report, or it will point to foods that are missing from our consumption basket, or even calculate the environmental footprint of all the food we eat.

Delivering Value in IOT

The IOT is one more interface for businesses, generating streams of data from physical environments. The IOT offers great fortunes for companies who will be bold enough to rethink their business models and honestly answer the question "what business are we in?"—allowing them to move from selling a product to delivering a composite service, which may include a physical product. It might even mean changing the commercial model where the product is only *leased* to the consumer who actually buys the service rather than acquire an asset.

Undoubtedly, the IOT is a big deal. We're talking about billions of connected devices changing the way we live our everyday lives. The transformative potential of this can barely be imagined. This will make a big difference to the way we deal with the sustainability, caring for an aging population, or getting supplies more efficiently to the needy, across the world. Although, there may be ongoing debate about whether our kettle should gossip with our washing machine! Meanwhile, I continue to dream about smart, connected windows, which can deliver safety, sunshine, and comfort to my home. As far as consumers are concerned, the I in IOT should really stand for *invisible technology*.

Tip: Ask how things could do different things than what they were originally designed for. What could a table do apart from being a flat surface? What could a roof be apart from the protection to your home?

CHAPTER 6

DiPhy or Phygital?

Redefining Reality

When Case, the protagonist of Gibson's 1984 novel *Neuromancer* jacks himself into the *cyberspace*, he embodies the paradigm that has always defined the way we see the digital world. There is a clear distinction between the real or physical world and the online world. The online world may be prosaic and made up of lines of typed text in a chat room—embellished at best by fonts and emojis, or it may be a virtual three-dimensional (3D) world such as was attempted by Second Life, and promised to us as the metaverse, by Facebook. Or in the realms of imagination—in literature and movies, such as *Avatar*, it may be a very lifelike environment with its own set of social and physical rules. This distinction has led us to some useful and not so useful phenomena. On the one hand, it has allowed us to escape ourselves and become different people, or even animals and other creatures. It has allowed us to explore what it would be like to be someone else, or something else. On the other hand, this has given us anonymous online trolling. But in the main, the distinction between real and online worlds has continued.

But as we speak, this wall is crumbling. We are finding ever-smarter ways of combining our digital and physical worlds. The smartphone allows us to control our environments ever more creatively, through sensors, and mixed reality—a combination of augmented reality (AR) and virtual reality (VR). VR actually harks back to the digital divide—as it transports us into an imaginary environment. But VR is so immersive that it is able to fool our brains into believing we are there. In future, VR may provide more physical and haptic inputs to make things even more real. Projects such as the metaverse from Facebook will attempt to bring the real world into the virtual—you and you colleagues might find yourselves interacting in this world doing real work, designing real products, which might be 3D printed in the real world at the end of your design workshop. AR is the opposite—layering the virtual on the real world. Imagine that a theologist, an architect, and an artist visit the Sistine Chapel. With AR, they may get fundamentally different experiences. The architect may be able to discover the minutiae of how it was built. With her AR glasses, she may notice the strengthening of the walls and how the dome is supported. The artist may be presented with a detailed view of the various stages of Michelangelo's work. The theologist may immerse herself in the interpretation of all the images.

You could even argue that Google Maps is a very good implementation of digital–physical thinking. You can identify where you are, and see the information overlay. And right on cue, Google has now introduced AR into their maps—you can hold up the map in the directions mode, and it will show you where to go based on the cityscape in front of you.

As with everything else in this section of the book, this is yet another interface. One more way for us to engage with software. One more way for software to connect with the world. And therefore, for a business, one more interface between your enterprise and its environment. As you start to encounter and use any of these tools—AR, VR, or their combination—often clubbed together as mixed reality (MR or XR) solutions, the additional layers of value will come from the data streams that emerge from these interactions and ensure that they are valued and used for optimizing the experience and ultimately the business model.

Some people call it *phygital*—this blending of physical and digital worlds. I prefer *di-phy*. Either way, welcome to the new reality.

Tip: Think about what information would make it easier to deal with the things, the environment and the infrastructure around you.

Redefining Computers

Computers are mutating as we speak. In common usage, a computer would typically refer to a home or office desktop computer, which includes a screen, keyboard, a processing unit, storage memory, and a mouse. The mouse vanished with the laptop. Storage was outsourced to the cloud. The processor and battery shrunk till you could fit a very powerful computer into the size of a phone. And very clearly, a combination of emerging technologies will push that still further—the screen and keyboard may vanish (think Amazon Echo), the computer itself may take many forms. A cylinder, a puck, a disc, or a cube. Equally, it might be a chair, a picture frame, or a jacket. Many of these may not be general purpose computers, but rather designed for specific tasks. Armed with a processor, connectivity, and controls, a smart chair might configure its contours for your comfort, or it might evaluate your sitting posture or monitor your resting heartbeat. Or all of the above, as apps.

One of the directions for the evolution of computing is the nano chip—which can be tiny particles–taking the form of a smart surface or coating. A paint-like layer that you can put on a wall, which will monitor weather conditions, check for environmental pollution, monitor sunlight, or change color and reflectivity to modulate insulation with changes in the temperature. The fact is, our entire world will be populated by smarter objects. From furniture and clothes, to pavements and homes. Therefore, everything will be an interface. A point of interaction.

It doesn't even have to be a computer. Increasingly, smarter materials can be meshed with computers to create entirely new architectures, environments, and tools. Graphene, for example, has been around for a while—the world's first two-dimensional (2D) material, 200 times stronger than steel, thinner than a human hair, and an excellent conductor. It is being used in next-generation screens, transistors, and possibly in the future as a semiconductor. Neri Oxman's work at the MIT Media Lab is all about combining materials and engineering with biology and art. She uses digital morphogenesis—a term that basically means that a material's properties vary depending on the context. Oxman calls this *Material Ecology*. Her projects include visionary ideas such as 3D printed wearable skins, which facilitate biological processes designed to help with inter-planetary travel. For example, the material can change densities based on the environment and gravitational force on different planets in the solar system. The material is also designed to house living organisms capable of producing oxygen. Her work includes the use of substances like chitin—which is the world's second most abundant bio-polymer, and can be sourced from the shells discarded by sea food restaurants, for example.

Tip: If an everyday object that you use could be smart and behave like a smart or living thing—what would you make it do?

Redefining Manufacturing

You could argue that 3D printing by itself is not really a *digital* technology, innovative though it is. Yet, if you consider its component pieces, it involves delivering design information or data to the printer so that a product can be created at the point of use. This takes out the entire supply chain, and also enables customization. You can see its value in 3D printed custom designed prosthetics. 3D printing is also called additive manufacturing—which means that unlike most traditional manufacturing, which involves removing material from a block to get a desired shape, 3D printing builds it from a spec, so there is no wastage of material either. The new cross rail (Queen Elizabeth Line) project in London that connects Heathrow and the western corridor to central London, uses 3D printed concrete slabs to reduce the effort of transporting them. In future, when we combine smart materials with 3D printers, you should be able to print a coffee mug to your own spec. By which I mean that its heat conducting properties may vary in a way you can define. Or its ability to change color if the sugar content of your drink is more than a specified amount, for instance. Additive manufacturing printing is especially useful with components that have complex shapes, or are not solid, as this requires molds and machining, which only work at scale.

Tip: Think about being able to print to order any shape whenever something breaks, so you can immediately fix it with a replacement part.

CHAPTER 7

The Human Interface

Voice and Language

"How will I live without Alexa?" a genuine question from my 10-year-old daughter while we were moving home earlier this year. She is proof that voice will be a central part of the human–digital interface. Not just because of what it can do already, that is book a cab, play your music, turn up the heating, or add items to your shopping list, but because of what its potential is. The simplicity of a voice interaction is seductive, whether you use Alexa, Siri, Cortana, Google Talk, or any other voice assistant.

There are many challenges with the current version of many of these technologies—for example, most voice assistants don't recognize voices. Consequently, they react to all voices, including those from the television in your house. In a strange meta moment, I've seen it react to itself. There was the day I asked Alexa for the news. After covering sports news, it moved to an Economist podcast about the CES (the Consumer Electronics Show, in Las Vegas), where they were talking about voice technologies. Including Alexa. And every time they used examples of questions for Alexa, my Alexa would try and answer them even though the questions were coming from the same Dot device. Finally, as the moderator in the news story said "Alexa, stop," my Alexa device turned itself off, and that was the end of the news program for me.

Despite these apparent shortcomings, we are at this point today because an incredible amount of complexity can now be handled by natural language processing tools, using artificial intelligence, neural networks, and much more. Lesser known companies like Nuance, recently acquired by Microsoft, continue to work on the engineering of the voice for specific uses such as health care. Beyond playing songs and ordering taxis, the real value of voice interaction might be for older people unable to handle a mobile or computer screen, or as a form of identity and authentication, or even as the interface to the world of ambient computing, driven by the IOT.

> Tip: Think of all the situations where vision is impaired, or the use of one's hands and fingers is restricted for any reason, so voice commands might be the most appropriate way of interacting with a system.

You ARE the Interface

The Gesture

Having owned the gaming industry with its GameBoy console in the late 1980s and 1990s, the team at Nintendo was clearly dismayed at losing out to Microsoft Xbox and the Sony Play Station by the turn of the century and the early 2000s. Nintendo needed a *game* changer. But instead of joining the arms race of memory, graphics, and processor power for the gaming consoles, Nintendo went a different way. The Nintendo Wii used motion sensing and a much more basic processor to create an entirely new casual gaming segment. The Wii audience was mostly families, who enjoyed the physical game experience, and adults who didn't have the time for the Xbox and PSP games. The Wii console turned Nintendo's fortunes around for the next five years. But it also set of a new category of interfaces. Others such as Kinect from Microsoft took this further. In 2009, a young man named Pranav Mistry acquired international stardom when he delivered a Ted talk based on the work he was doing at the MIT on the Sixth Sense technology—which provided glimpses of how the future of computing could do away with the screen and keyboard, in favor of a wearable device and gestures. It is very likely that the next-generation users will treat the screen and keyboard as only one of the many ways of interacting with computers that continue to blend with their environment.

> Tip: What are the conditions under which speaking or using a keyboard may be difficult—perhaps due to the ambient noise, where gestures are the most effective way of interaction?

The Body

Amanda is chatting with Ravi. This scene from five years ago has stuck in my head. Amanda Boxtel's legs have been paralyzed for 25 years. She has just delivered a session, which she starts in a wheel chair but completes walking around the stage strapped into a robot-like exoskeleton. She has worked with many major exoskeleton providers, but her key complaint is that they still look like robots—she would prefer hers to look like an evening dress. We're not there yet, but it has become a lot more intelligent. For example, it senses her movements and helps her to complete a step forward. Yet, it doesn't just do it for her because it has been trained to help her with her therapy, so it ensures that she puts the right amount of effort in as well. After her season, she is standing around in her *clunky but smart* exoskeleton, talking to my colleague Ravi. He isn't actually there, though it's a *face-to-face* conversation. Ravi is using a *telepresence* robot—which allows him to drive a 5 ft. tall device on wheels through the conference area, with his face at *eye level* on an iPad sized screen, and through this, converse with people he meets. Ravi is actually in New York, but could be anywhere in the world. This conversation—a bionics meets robotics scene—is imprinted on my mind as vision for the future.

> Tip: What are all the ways in which you would augment human capabilities—either to restore physical functions or to enhance them?

The Brain

The human brain has become much less mysterious than ever before. Telekinesis was for the longest time beyond the reach of physics. But that was when we saw it as a power of thought. Now we see the granular circuitry and understand the physics and chemistry of the brain, and suddenly we're able to make that leap. And not just any leap—how about flying a plane with brain signals? By connecting *Wired Magazine* journalist Jack Stewart's brain to the plane—essentially through a skull cap and electrodes, Honeywell has demonstrated that it's possible for a person with no flying experience to maneuver a plane just by directed thought. Note, we're still not talking about being able to wave an arm and have our biscuit tin fly to us across the room. But if the biscuit tin had the means to fly and needed the instructions, we could, in future, do so just by thinking about it. Think about all the things that we operate via instructions—from the TV to the coffee machine. It's possible that we will in future be able to issue those instructions just by thinking about them in specific ways. In 2017, Elon Musk announced Neuralink—his venture for connecting artificial intelligence (AI) to the brain. Stentrode, a competitor to Neuralink, has started clinical trials in Australia. Stentrode focuses on neuroprosthesis, a way to restore functional independence to people suffering from paralysis.

Bio-Electronics

In 2016, I heard a talk delivered by a scientist from Galvani Bioelectronics—a GSK-Alphabet joint venture—talking about their alternative approach to tackling long-term conditions. This research initiative is eschewing the traditional *chemical*-based approach, which works on the basis that the whole body gets exposed to the medication, but only the targeted organ responds. This is a *blunt instrument*. Instead, the new approach takes a *bio-electronic* approach, which will use an electronic approach to target individual nerves and control the impulses they send to the affected organ, say the pancreas, for diabetes patients. This will be done through nanotechnology and by inserting a *rice grain*-sized chip via keyhole surgery. A successful administration of this medicine will potentially ensure that the patient no longer has to worry about taking pills on time, or even monitoring the insulin levels, as the nano-device will do both monitoring and control of insulin levels.

YOU are the Interface

We tend to assume that is a clear interface between human and machine, made of physical components and software. But as the example of voice interfaces suggests, in the future when computers are embedded into everything, much more human interfaces may be optimal. We will see ever more ways for us to manage computers and equally more ways for computers to help us, or even *fix* us. You may find this exciting or creepy, but a vision of us as cyborgs is certainly one of the scenarios that emerge.

But as you can well appreciate, this entirely new interface will throw up a mountain of opportunities and data, but equally, a whole universe of new questions around ethics, regulations, privacy, theft, security, and others. Consequently, it will transform industries from health care to insurance to media, retail, law, and policing. In the first instance, it will redefine how we interact with computers. From the traditional screen and keyboard model to a voice and no-screen environment, through to just gestures and even thought. But once we've gotten over that, we'll start to look at all the new data this generates. For one, it will expand the range of contexts under which we can interact with computers. Without overly taxing our multitasking skills or causing danger, we will be able to interact with a computer while cooking or driving. Many of these interactions will happen even without us being consciously involved, as in the case of the pharmaceutical example or the working of exoskeletons. Second, it will open up an entirely new chapter on data—as this data will be even more voluminous, and raise more questions on privacy, protection and use. Third, it will allow us to redefine our life choices, social mores structures, and allow us to optimize our very lives based on the data generated. For example, voice analysis will inform us about when our stress levels are highest. Perhaps we will be surprised to learn that we are more stressed while driving on motorways. Or that a particular condition that is triggered by stress flares up under those conditions, allowing us to make different choices about when and how we drive.

As our natural interfaces grow, there may come a point where we may struggle to distinguish between where we end and the computer begins. This is one of the facets of singularity, proposed by Ray Kurzweil. But that's a discussion for another day!

CHAPTER 8

Why Is Good Design So Difficult?

Both Loud and Versatile

In the early 19th century, a Belgian boy called Adolphe Sax came to be known as "little Sax, the ghost" because of the number of times he survived brushes with disaster. He swallowed a pin, he burnt his side on a cast iron hot frying pan, survived suffocation from fumes from the varnish kept in his room, and even managed to singe himself in a gunpowder explosion. No doubt these experiences gave him a zest for life, as he went on to join his parents' business in making musical instruments and proceeded to invent and innovate a number of horns, flutes, and clarinets. In 1846 he patented his most famous invention—the saxophone. The saxophone is not just one of the most recent instruments to be created, but it has a recognized inventor and a clear date of invention, whereas most instruments have evolved over time. Guitars, for example, go back thousands of years. The saxophone was designed to be as powerful as the brass instruments—such as trumpets—but have the variety and subtlety of woodwind instruments—such as flutes. Note the use of the word designed—as a set of conscious choices. A bamboo reed vibrates when the saxophone is played to originate the sound. The brass body acts as an amplifying column, but the shape of the brass body ensures that the overtones are octaves. This is key to the ease of finger work on a saxophone. A standard tenor saxophone has 23 keys—including closed standing keys—which open when pressed, and open standing keys, which work in reverse. Sax originally launched 14 versions of his instrument—playing at various different keys, although a couple of them went on to become the most popularly used ones (E-Flat and B-Flat, since you ask).

What stands out though was that Sax had a clear idea of what outcome he wanted to create. He would have had to experiment with hundreds of options—keeping in mind this was the mid-1800s, so this would not have been an easy process. He would have had to master the metal work, the acoustics, the mechanics, and the ergonomics. Ultimately, people would need to play the instrument, and if they couldn't hold it or work the keys, it would be useless. A number of significant additions have been made to the design of the saxophone, but Sax's original invention is a great example of how a good design works. He had specific sets of users in mind—for example, military bands—who often had to play in environments where they needed to be heard over other sounds. Later, the saxophone would get an entirely new life as the distinctive sound of jazz. This is another common feature of great inventions and design—they often transcend uses and become a conduit for innovation.

Digital Demands Living Design

Today, we live in a world that has been overtaken by digital. Our content, art, music, money, and our conversations have all gone digital. This digitization means that it has become much easier to create, curate, distribute, and copy. There is a fluidity in digital that simply did not exist in the physical world. Our attention spans have grown smaller, leading to a corresponding pithiness in our communication. Moreover, the digital space is continuously evolving and upgrading. New hardware, operating systems, tools, methodologies mean that nothing can be built and then just allowed to be. It must be reworked, updated, and continuously modified. It's a whole universe away from Adolphe Sax's world of musical instruments, which would be painstakingly designed and created over a decade and then survive over centuries with modifications every 20 years or so, which means in this high-speed, constant changing world of digital, we must make those active choices consistently, repeatedly, and often objectively reframe the question. Even if you had the best web-based banking product, you had to ask different questions when it came to redesigning it for mobiles. And even if it was perfect for mobiles, you had to rethink it for tablets. One of the biggest changes today is that design, like development, needs to become a continuous and ongoing activity—a kind of living design endeavor.

> Tip: Pick any activity and think of how that activity (end to end) has changed over the past 10 years for you—either because you've changed or because the interfaces have changed.

Change and Constancy

This doesn't take away the value of consistency in design. We need to make things better, not different. The temptation to repeatedly reinvent too many aspects of a product or its interface can leave people feeling tired and confused. Over the course of its life as a Microsoft Offering, very rarely have tools like Word and Excel significantly overhauled interface and interaction design. You can recognize much of the icons in the Windows 95 version of Word, but if you're like me, you probably still curse when the current version of office doesn't follow some abstruse keystroke sequence you liked to use. Google took 15 years of tinkering to arrive at its single clean landing page. We still use the point-and-click user interface that was originally created by Xerox in the 1970s and popularized by Apple's Macintosh and then Microsoft Windows. This means that all the continuous evolution we do also needs to allow for an underlying consistency of the design. This is definitely one of the harder challenges in a fast-changing digital world—when change becomes easy, it's more important to know what to keep constant, not what to change.

The Order of Conscious Choices

Every time I see street artists do portraits or caricatures of people, as they do in Leicester Square in London or in town centers in many major cities, I always have this strange joke running in my head about standing behind the person and getting painted into the picture. A ridiculous idea, of course. You can photobomb a selfie or any photograph, but you can't photobomb a painting. Every brushstroke of a painting is a conscious decision. Even the white space is a choice. Nothing is there without the active will of the painter. Design is similar—everything is a choice.

As Irene Au, the Design Head at Khosla Ventures, said, there's nothing such as *no design*—it's either thoughtful design or careless design. The design challenges are different, but some of the principles are still the same. At the heart of design is conscious choice. Seen in this light, design is perhaps the act of asking and answering the why behind anything that is produced by people. Design thinking takes this a bit further and tries to address when that question should be raised. Especially when it comes to the world of technology and digital products.

Historically, a lot of technology and software creation followed three broad phases. First, some business people agreed on what the key functionalities were going to be. Business analysts and consultants would meticulously capture encyclopedic volumes of requirements to this effect. The technology team would build the software based on some order defined by the analysts, and finally, some designers would be called in to beautify the screens—aka the UI. This was fundamentally true for business applications but also for a lot of products. A part of the reason was the technology was clunky, the functionality was difficult to stitch together, delivering performance in terms of speed and reliability was hard, and it was fundamentally simpler to define how the software would work and get people to follow the software model. This is not uncommon—early stage technologies often focus on functionality—from the "any color as long as it's black" philosophy of the Ford Model T, all the way to the glass-hole version of the Google Glass. That world has flipped in the past decade, thanks to a number of concurrent evolutionary trends. Agile methods, reliable open-source software, RESTful API design and modular architectures (all of these are covered later in this book)—these are just some of the drivers of the new model we see today. The biggest impact of all these, taken collectively, and the reason why digital platforms are so widely adopted is that they enable the technology to adapt to human behavior, rather than the reverse model described earlier. This means, first, that we now start with design and understanding the user and this becomes the critical input to the functionality to be built along with any functional blocks that are considered essential to delivering this experience, and the technology delivers to this ask. This is a revolutionary idea that many technology companies have struggled to culturally adapt to. And arguably, the reason why most businesses have tended to work with digital agencies with good design skills, side by side with large systems integrators for technology execution. When I built a design team within my mobile solutions team for a global technology firm, the biggest challenge was getting my colleagues to understand the value of this design unit, although our clients understood and appreciated it immediately. Even now, a simple test for any digital provider is to ask about the ratio of designers to developers or analysts in any team!

A second implication of this switch is that we can now allow people to choose their preferred way of interacting with the system and allow for multiple user behaviors for the same functionality within the system. A mature digital retailer can allow each customer to start their shopping journey on any platform—Web, mobile, in store, on the phone—and continue this journey through any other platform without the basic functionality breaking. You would have heard the word omnichannel on a number of occasions, but its efficacy depends critically on design thinking—which means putting the user at the center and building process and technology around her needs.

> Tip: For any new digital product or project, start by constructing the map of stakeholders, and considering the needs and success criteria for each of the stakeholders.

The Science of Design

Dieter Rams famously constructed the 10 principles of good design 40 years ago, and they still hold true. He talked about design being innovative, detailed, honest, easy to understand, and my personal favorite—as little design as possible. What he didn't mention was the means to get to those end states. Design thinking offers us that path. It actually presents design as a science rather than an art. Design thinking is in effect, the science of design—it relies on continuous cycles of observation, inference, hypothesis and testing, with the user at the center of this cycle.

It's a cliché to say we put the user in the center, but that by itself is a difficult ask. It requires a number of skills and choices. Objectivity, empathy, observation, persistence, patience—all of these are key to the task of the design thinker. Getting rid of your baggage of assumptions is harder than it sounds. When we were designing early websites, one of my favorite exercises used to be to half of a group of people to agree on what they would put on the home page of a pizza delivery store, and for the other half to think of what they'd like to see as customers. Invariably, the pizza makers would want to first talk about their quality, ingredients and customer service, while the customers group would first want to know opening hours, address, and phone details, and whether they delivered home. Often, the very questions you ask may be the wrong ones. This is why, observation rather than question and answer is seen as the preferred option. Especially because more often than not, you're designing new services and innovative products for which the user has no reference or perhaps even need. This is the reason for the classic quote ascribed to Henry Ford who is supposed to have said "If I asked my customers what they wanted, they would have said faster horses." Ford was both right and wrong, as it turns out. He was right to not ask customers the blunt question, instead relying on his observation that people were ready to upgrade to a different form of transport. But he was wrong to ignore them altogether and paid for his hubris when a decade later, General Motors pulled the proverbial rug from under the feet of Ford Motors by providing what the market wanted—which included installment purchases, used car trade-ins, and more choices. The trick therefore is not to get it right once, but to make a habit of validating your hunches through observed behavior. A few decades later, Honda sent a team of researchers to the United States. One set of researchers spent a whole afternoon in the parking lot of Disneyland observing what people put in the boots of their cars, and in what order things went in and out, so that they could design the boot of the car appropriately. When was the last time you put that level of thought and detail into building something?

It's clear that this approach has always been there, in a lot of product designs—especially for automobiles, and other high-value goods. We are in a way returning to those product design principles today because we've had to think beyond the interface. In the world of the Web, we just had to worry about the browser and so design had become synonymous with UI design—the interface, or the screen real estate was all that mattered. Today, we need to think about so much more—for example, the shape and size of the phone, relative to the size of a person's hands. Whether she might be standing, sitting, driving, or walking. We need to think about what happens before or after the screens are used. In fact, when I speak with designers nowadays, I'm always curious to understand how they see the future of design as we move to a world beyond screens. In a world of IOT, robots, and voice interfaces, we are no longer designing the UI or even the UX around a screen. We are soon going to be designing interactions, experiences, and environments. These may include a screen but will definitely be more immersive and require a lot more than screen design. This is one of the reasons why we're back in the world of product design—a lot of this may involve tactile, haptic, and perhaps even olfactory interfaces in future, and associated feedback. They may involve spatial and sensory aspects of design. They may require a grasp of materials and their capability—especially with new smart materials such as graphene, in the mix. Apple's designers were known to work with both interfaces and materials to ensure they are cohesive in their thinking. As technology expands the world of possibilities, the designers of tomorrow need to find the golden space between users' unmet needs and our ability to solve for them.

Tip: While working on a digital project, start by constructing a set of assumptions—even very basic ones—which will need to hold true for your product to work. See what happens if you tweak or change those assumptions.

Marrying Observation With Data

One of the challenges of the observational approach is that it doesn't scale well. How many individuals can you study in depth? You may be lucky enough to design something like a wayfinding system at an airport, for which you're able to simultaneously study the movement and behavior of a large number of people. But in most cases, for example, people buying airline tickets, you can only observe a few in real life. This is where digital design leaps ahead. Once we've connected our users to a digital interface, be it Web or mobile, we start to be able to *observe* their behavior through their interactions, which comes to us through data. We may not be able to see all their choice related discussions, but this is more than adequately made up by the fact that the data tells us what explicit choice they did make and also what mini-choices they made along the way. For example, we know that this family viewed four different locations in Greece before settling on a specific location such as the island of Kos, and we can see they have booked flights to Kos. We can even see that in each location, they looked at hotels and particularly, swimming pools and bars. What's more, we have this granularity for every single user on the platform. What we lose in the depth of each observation, we make up by the volume of observed choice making across the entire universe of users. This point is covered in more detail in the chapter on data, but getting design and data to work together is often where the magic happens.

> Tip: Fine-tune design choices by validating with data as early as possible.

The Role of the Designer in a Data-Driven World

Does this mean that every decision has to be made on the basis of data? Google famously user-tested 40 shades of blue by exposing 2.5 percent of their visitors to each shade and checking people's reaction to the shade. There are plenty of arguments as to why this might be overkill. But the more important point is that there are bigger and more directional choices that are harder to test at such levels of granularity, especially ones that don't involve pixels on a screen. The shape of a car, the layout of a bank branch, or the usability of a machine tool—these can't be tested over and over in the same way that elements on a screen can. This is where a designer's experience and direction are critical. Note that this is not an argument for doing away with user testing or validation. We are simply highlighting the role of the designer in the process. Consider these two scenarios— first, given enough time, can you start with just a jumble of pieces on a page and A/B test your way to a great website? This is the equivalent of the monkey with the typewriter producing the works of Shakespeare. Clearly, nobody has that infinite amount of time. Second, if all design is data driven, then for a given industry or segment, all design should lead to the same end point—that is, all sites competing for the same audiences would end up as mirrors of each other. Obviously, both of these are examples of reductio ad absurdum—only intended to highlight the critical contribution of the design expert. Erika Hall covers this well when she talks about philosophy being an essential design skill. There is certainly a directional impetus, a subjective view and occasionally a counterintuitive perspective, which is key to us creating new worlds and new ideas—things that cannot be built through popularity.

> Tip: Be aware of the limitations of volume data, use design for the big ideas and counter-intuitive thinking.

The Power of Design Thinking

Look around your desk, your home or your world—design is everywhere. You're likely to notice some great design, a lot of average design, and occasionally poor design. The power of good design needs no convincing—it creates memorability (Volkswagen Beetle), elicits a strong emotional response (Apple iPhone), and becomes a mainstay of our lives (the classic table lamp or Levis Jeans). But even at an organizational level, the difference design makes can be stark. The Design Management Institute tracks a set of companies in a *Design Value Index*—these are companies chosen for their focus on design. The set of companies is periodically refreshed with entries and exits. This set of companies has outperformed the S&P Index over the past 10 years by 200 percent. You may well ponder the causation versus correlation aspects of this analysis, but it's intuitively sensible that companies that drive better design through their products will do better than their competitors. This kind of systemic design improvement isn't down to hiring a designer, or even an army of designers, it's more about building a culture of design and bringing both the art and science of design to bear on your products and services and building the business around it. After all, if design is built around the user, and your business is built around design, then you are, by definition, a customer-centric business.

CHAPTER 9

What Is Service Design, and Why Is It Suddenly Sexy?

What Is Service Design?

Have you ever noticed that people who sell tangible products—such as cars or even clothes—focus on the intangibles or services their products will deliver, whereas people who sell services such as banks, often call their offerings *products*? In the continuum between products and services, almost every so-called product or service falls somewhere in the middle. Each offering, say a mortgage or a physiotherapy, is a product, in that it has some structure—by way of a price point, a benefit, a mode of delivery an underlying technology or principle, and a form—physical or digital. But every product is also a service—seen as the lifetime of value it delivers every time you use it. An electric iron provides the service of pressed clothes, and a saucepan provides the service of cooking—admittedly not by themselves, but you expect to extract that service over the lifetime of the product. In case of an actual service—this is easy to understand—if you're eating a meal at a restaurant or taking a train ride. For a product, this is a little harder to visualize and model. One way of looking at this service model is that the service is the sum total of your experiences with the product, and incorporates everything from how the product is initiated, used, consumed, updated, and even discarded.

Some of these words such as initiated and updated sound a bit like software terms. They are simply my convenient terms for which you're welcome to use alternatives. Before you actually use an item of furniture you may need to get it home, set it up or assemble it, move it around, and discard the packaging. A packet of sugar may require unsealing, transfer to a container, or resealing. As products go more digital—they will require to be connected to the power socket or charged, set up—which may include a Wi-Fi connection, and some initial instructions. All of this is the initiation—increasingly significant for digital products. And likewise, all products need an update from time to time—which may include cleaning, repair, maintenance work, but for digital, this could be software updates, and for complex products, it could involve replacement of parts.

Once you start thinking of products through their life cycle, you can understand why the idea of a layer of service applies to everything—from hotel rooms, to fountain pens. And when you think about designing— this brings to the forefront the notion of service design. When you apply it to products—you start to consider the entire set of life cycle experiences the product offers. When you apply it to services, you consider all the components that are responsible, including human interactions, infrastructure, computers, and physical environments. As a designer, when you take ownership of the experience, you take on a bigger task than simply focusing on the narrow product or service definition. When Lenny Riggio, the CEO of Barnes and Noble, suggested that one of his better decisions was to put toilets in his stores, he was inadvertently thinking service design. He wasn't just thinking about how people buy books— he was thinking of the entire experience of book browsing, and recognizing that often the call of nature is what would curtail a book browsing experience.

Tip: For your next digital project, instead of asking your end users, sit with them and see how they currently do the task or meet the need that you're designing a product for. Note all the points of dissatisfaction and where you think the experience could be improved.

So, Why Is Service Design Suddenly So Hot?

"Software is Eating the World." This quote by Marc Andreessen rings true, no matter what industry you look at. Every product and service we use, from health to automobiles is getting smarter. And increasingly, the value of the product or service is delivered by the software and code rather than the physical infrastructure. Everything is also getting connected.

And the combination of smart and connected can fundamentally reshape our interactions.

Technology Brings the Physical World to Life

The digital world is bringing our experiences to life in different and unique ways. What used to be just a poster or a hoarding for a coffee shop in an airport can now allow us to scan a coupon and get a discount if we use it within the next 30 minutes. So, instead of just noting the hoarding, we can actually engage with its message. A smart weighing scale not only tells us our weight but keeps a record of previous readings, shows us trends, perhaps identifies patterns in our weight that can be inferred by us, by the machine or by our doctors, who may be sent the data directly by the weighing scale. As you can see, these smarter products are reshaping our experience model. And we talked earlier about the service model being a sum of our experiences with a product. The onus is on us to design these experiences.

Use, Not Own

One of the outcomes of digital models is the emergence of the sharing economy. As with everything else, there is probably more hype than reality about what can be shared. But we've already seen examples of how we can start to rent assets to each other in more meaningful ways. Spare rooms and second homes can be put on Airbnb (or even your own home if you're away for a week, as many do). You can rent your car parking space, or rent yourself along with your car. Conversely, you can use a car without buying it via car clubs, to the extent that car companies are actively experimenting with this model including Daimler, Audi, BMW, and GM. (We also call these XaaS models, later in the book.)

These changes bring new challenges. Creating new service wrappers around existing products; adding entirely new layers of value and complexity; enabling new behaviors that have no reference or benchmark but need to be intuitive to use; and managing the complex life cycle of these products and services across multiple interfaces, touch points, and data considerations. It's impossible to think of solving for all of this without service design principles being followed.

Tip: Pick any product and think of the service you expect it to deliver to you over the course of its life. How could the service be made better?

How Does Service Design Work?

Service design involves applying the same design principles of observation, empathy, detail, and completeness to a service experience. By definition, it forms a kind of cocreation between the designer and the user. A service design map may chart out the entire *journey* a user makes in consuming a service. In this case, a service could mean using the TV you just bought, using an app to get directions, or depositing money at a bank. It needs to be contextual and take into account the environmental factors and emotional state of the user. Often it also involves creating an ecosystem of people and entities involved in delivering and consuming the service.

Service design methods can expose the fallacy of our ingrained assumptions as well as provide fundamental insights. When my team was working at a major airport, we conducted a detailed user journey analysis as a part of a service design exercise. We constructed a set of personas: for example, a family with two kids, a backpacker, an executive traveler, and so on. We looked at every step and interaction from passport control to baggage X-ray, to gate and boarding. One of the biggest insights I remember the team came up with from this exercise was that people didn't really care about the airport. The airport team was keen to curate a great experience and brand message. But for most travelers, the airport is incidental. Perhaps a good analogy is the referee in a football game. If the referee is doing a good job, you don't notice him. In the same way, travelers were focused on their destination, and the airport would be doing its job well if they didn't notice the airport. This changed the entire design of the app to refocus the experience on the destination, rather than the airport.

What Is a "Good" Service Design?

Designers shooting for usable is like a chef shooting for edible.

—@Ky4ep (Twitter)

Usability should be the very entry criteria for any design effort. Yet you can see examples all around that fall short of this. Packaging that won't open, a cap that once open won't close. A pen with a bad grip, a confusing website, we see this stuff every day. But service design fails are also those that haven't thought through the entire life cycle of the product experience. You may have a great app, but it takes 20 minutes to download over Wi-Fi. Or an amazing device, but it takes a PhD in computer science to set up. The actual implementation of good service design can be achieved through all aspects of the service—including software, hardware, design, infrastructure, materials used, and more. Every time a complex thing is made easy—like navigating the London Underground using Harry Beck's famous 1931 design—you know you've achieved good service design.

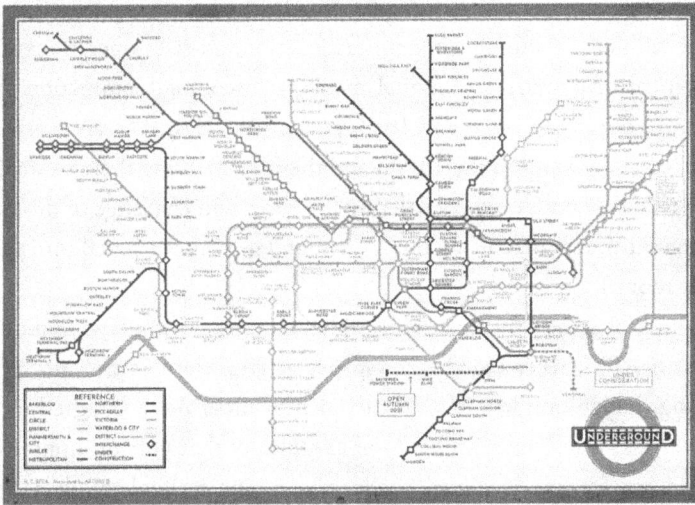

Figure 9.1 London Tube Map, 1931, by Harry Beck

Simplicity—A Fiendishly Difficult Problem

The holy grail of almost every product and service is simplicity. After all, nobody sets out to create a complicated experience. Yet, it remains beyond the reach of many. There are many definitions for simplicity. Mostly, they revolve around being basic, or easy to use, or intuitive, doing things that bring calm. In the Indian mythological epic Mahabharata, *Yudhishthir* was so named because he could be calm (*shthir*), in battle (*yudh*). We find simplicity easy to recognize. Whether it's a home-cooked meal, or the joy of a sunset, our favorite beverage consumed in our favorite chair. In products, intuitiveness is a good test—that is, something that does not require education, training, or a manual. In their own ways, both Nokia and iPhone have displayed this kind of intuitive simplicity. The commercial power of simplicity is also obvious. Simplicity drives acceptance and adoption. It is the reason why soccer is the world's favorite game, or why the World Wide Web is indeed worldwide. Simplicity for many people is a deeply held philosophy.

The next time when you switch on your TV set at the end of a long week and settle in to watch prime time sports, all you'll need to do is switch on the TV, the set top box, and find the right channel. But for the broadcaster, the process may have started almost a year before. In fact, considering the complexity of a broadcast operation—including all the scheduling, planning, program acquisition, ad-sales operations, the movement of physical and digital media, transcoding, automation and transmission, compliance and legal, and other areas, it is an everyday miracle that you switch the TV on and there's something there to watch. (And this is without even considering the effort and challenge of producing the show, manufacturing the TV set, and getting the signal into your living room.)

Think of some of your other simple examples—withdrawing money from an ATM, receiving the newspaper at your door in the morning, turning the ignition key in your car; each of these and a hundred more simple tasks often mask an ocean of complexity that goes on unnoticed behind the scenes. As digital products combine technology, data, and experiences in more and more sophisticated ways, this is the fundamental lesson of simplicity. Often, to make something simple, especially for an end user of a product or process, you have to take on and resolve an enormous amount of complexity. Nothing annoys me more than managers who cut short a complex discussion around a difficult problem with "we need to make this simple." Complexity doesn't vanish, it gets resolved, in great detail, by somebody else, and kept under the hood, so you can just turn a key or press a button to start a car. After all, as the writer HL Mencken said, "For every complex problem there is an answer that is clear, simple, and wrong."

Tip: Think of a simple thing like turning on the tap and drinking a glass of water. Try and draw a map of everything that needs to happen for you to be able to perform this simple task.

CHAPTER 10

Digital Infrastructure: Cloud

What do you call a sheep without legs?—A cloud!
—John Bishop and Jose Mourinho charity sketch.

Never mind the sheep, to think of a digital service today without a cloud-based architecture is like a table with a leg missing. To be fair, it's not just cloud, but the layer we should think of as *Digital infrastructure* or the invisible part of any digital solution. This includes cloud, middleware, and security. In this chapter, let's focus on cloud services.

What Is It?

The easiest way to think about cloud services is to think about computing power on tap. Just like electricity. You don't have to generate your own power, or have your own generator, for which you would have to determine up front how much power you would need and therefore what kind of generator to invest in. Our homes are connected to the national grid, and we just switch on our devices, consume the energy we need, and pay for the amount used. This is exactly what cloud computing has done for information technology (IT) infrastructure and servers. It converts the entire complexity of server hardware, operating systems, configurations, and all the ancillary services into a utility model and allows you to *pay as you go*.

History

The idea of accessing remote computers for processing power dates back to the days of mainframes, but cloud computing, as we know it today, can be traced back to the post dot.com crash period with startups trying to build more cost-efficient models for growth. Amazon was one of the survivors who built a significant cloud environment for its own needs, and in 2006, launched a service to allow other companies to use its cloud-based Web services. Over the next few years, Amazon Web Services (AWS) matured quickly to become enterprise-grade, and coupled with the emergence of open-source software, quickly became a de facto standard for new applications being built and run at a small fraction of their precursors.

Today, the top three providers—AWS, Microsoft (Azure) and Google Cloud Platform (GCP)—are collectively known as the hyper-scalers. The global scale and performance of businesses such as Netflix, which accounts for 40 percent of the total U.S. Internet traffic has also bolstered the confidence of corporations. Nobody really questions the cloud model anymore. The default position for most large businesses is (a) multi-cloud—using more than one provider, and (b) hybrid cloud models—which means a combination of private and public cloud providers.

Meanwhile, the explosion of personal and enterprise apps and web-based consumer businesses ensured that whether or not you thought you actively considered the cloud, you're using the cloud every time you use stream music or video, use Gmail or Google Maps, use Zoom or Teams, book a taxi on Ola, or plan your next holiday on TripAdvisor.

Why?

The most critical part of the cloud's advantage is the flexibility. A digital project almost by definition is not likely to work to long-term projections cast in stone. The proposition, the product or app, the commercial model, may all change during the lifetime of the solution, and even over the course of the delivery of the project. Consequently, the idea that your infrastructure can grow and shrink with your needs, and services be turned on and off as required is like oxygen for the project. In the precloud era, a significant amount of cost and time would be spent on infrastructure, planning, and sizing. And that was often the largest capital commitment and risk. Now it's a flow that you can turn on and off. And you can spend all that planning time and energy on your core business.

Even better, you can ramp down as well as up. You can set up a test bed for your alpha service, shut it down, and build a new one for Beta. This allows you to convert a lot of your capital expenditure (CapEx) to operational expenditure (OpEx), which is in essence healthier as it keeps pace with your revenue and operational scale.

It's worth bearing in mind that the reason firms with a small operational footprint can scale globally and quickly is because of the power of the cloud, and the ability to deliver a customized service almost anywhere in the world and manage it with a small and remote team. And because new servers and entire platforms can be spun up at short notice, even programmatically, you can respond to spikes in demand almost instantly.

The XAAS Model

We spoke earlier of the conversion of infrastructure into a utility model, available on tap and on a pay as you go basis. Another way of describing this is to call it infrastructure as a service. You don't pay to own your own infrastructure, you pay to rent it *as a service*. You can now rent infrastructure, software, or entire platforms using this model. This is generically known as the *XaaS* model. The *aaS* here means *as a Service*—and X can be applied to software (SaaS), infrastructure (IaaS), or platforms (PaaS). As a simple analogy, you might say that owning a car is like the old world of buying and owning your infrastructure, whereas a car club is a *car as a service*, and a taxi is a *ride as a service* model.

Containerization

You may come across this term while building an ecommerce application or a mobile app. Containerization is a relatively recent innovation in the application infrastructure environment. The term comes from the shipping industry where the use of standardized containers across the world allowed everybody to speak the same language and measures while shipping goods. It gave the entire industry a common unit of shipping goods. In the same way, containerization in the application space allows for the definition of a number of aspects of the server environment in which the application runs. Docker is one of the companies that was an early player in the containerization space.

Bringing Functionality to Content/Data

One of the innovative ideas from Amazon Web Services (AWS) came from the insight that while content is often very heavy and unwieldy to move around, the actual operations people want to perform on the content by themselves are much more lightweight. This led to the idea that rather than move content around in a workflow, it would be much easier to keep the content in one place and allow all the operations to be performed on the content. This could for example include adding audio descriptions, editing, encoding, and reformatting, for video content. Today, this model is being adopted by many others. For example, if you store documents on Dropbox, you can edit a PowerPoint presentation without downloading it from Dropbox, or the Microsoft Office 365 Cloud. Multiple people can access the same version and make their edits. This kind of shared workspace model is a key benefit of cloud-based environments, and it points to the cloud as a virtual shared workspace, rather than just storage.

Do You Need Your Own Cloud Strategy?

As a business user or owner, you shouldn't usually have to create your own cloud strategy unless you're launching a completely new digital product. Your organization or your CIO probably has a cloud strategy already with one or more hyper-scaler. Don't be surprised, though, if there are a few AWS or Azure accounts floating around between your development teams or in the IT organization. You should probably avoid the easy route of just using a credit card and setting up another cloud account because over time, this becomes an inefficient model at scale. At least check with your IT organization about existing cloud accounts you can use.

You will definitely need to understand the cost structures and what you're paying for, but don't forget what you're saving in the process. Most cloud providers have dozens of services with individual prices and easy-to-use calculators to predict the cost outflows. You should keep in mind that the cloud is no longer just about storage or hardware. Now, the entire ecosystem of your application servers, software, platforms, database, data, and the functionality of your system—all of it can live in the cloud.

Tip: Sit down with your lead developer and go through all the services you might need for your application and use the calculator to see what your needs and costs might look like under different scenarios.

CHAPTER 11

Digital Infrastructure: Middleware and API

For the first 14 years of its existence, Lego was a wooden toy maker. Then in 1946, Lego bought the first injection molding in Denmark, and spent the next 12 years, it persisted, through many setbacks, to create a model of plastic *bricks*, which would provide the optimum level of adhesion for children to snap them together and then pull them apart, without the bricks falling apart of their own volition. But once the stud and tube coupling system (look under a Lego brick) was patented in 1958, it did more than hold two pieces of plastic together. It allowed the creation of the Lego *brick architecture*—which allowed any two pieces of Lego to be snapped together. It made Lego a platform of toys. A platform on which the next 60 years of success has been built. Most importantly, it turned the entire world of Lego into components with standard interfaces. It added unbounded imagination to the constructive powers of Lego without having to worry about compatibility, and how the pieces would work together. And a six-year-old can pick any two of them and snap them together, and pull them apart.

The Many Problems of Connecting Software

It should be intuitively obvious at this point why the world of software doesn't work as elegantly as Lego, but here are four specific problems:

First, software is not an industrial, machine-made component. It's made by humans who apply their judgment at every stage of the process. Consequently, almost no two pieces of software are exactly the same. Imagine if Lego bricks were made by hand by people from all over the world!

Second, software is made by thousands of different companies. Even if individuals can be given a set of rules, each firm has its own set of guidelines and approaches to writing software. Although, the reality is that within most firms, there is no consistency, and for the most part, no historical need for consistency at a granular level in the way the software is actually written. And the processes of standardization are themselves like tides in the ocean, which come and go, as each company in the industry strives for unique value and defendable market positions. This is like trying to fit Lego bricks with Meccano pieces.

Third, the way software is designed, conceptualized, built, and run have all changed over the past few decades, and continues to evolve as we speak. The state-of-the-art software written 20 years ago bears little resemblance to today's code. We therefore often have the problem of backward compatibility—making sure new software can talk to old software. This is easier said than done, as the older systems may completely lack the ability to communicate efficiently, and may need expensive changes in order to be able to do so. This would be like fitting the plastic Lego pieces to the wooden ones, which were never designed to work that way.

Finally, there's the constant change that software deals with. A single piece of software—one functionality with a system—say that deals with applying tax to a product price—can go through many changes driven by the environment—including regulatory changes, business changes, competitive decisions, process changes, compliance requirements, or the impact of other software being introduced. Imagine that the Lego pieces lost their snap over time and repeated use.

For all these reasons, we can't simply assume that any two pieces of software will talk to each other, unless they are specifically designed to do so.

Why Does This Matter?

If you're doing something meaningful in the digital environment—you are likely to require access to information in your company's core systems (systems of record). You may need to change an existing core process, or update a record maintained in a key system. By this, I mean records that hold key information about customers, sales, prices, products, transactions, suppliers, or employees. Simple apps such as *checking balance* in a banking app or *view loyalty points* for an airline app or *make a proximity-based offer* for a retailer—all require this kind of backend system access. In the simplest case, you may just need to read information from those systems, but in more complex scenarios, you might be updating or adding to the data in the core systems.

Typically, this is the point at which your digital project needs the support of your IT team. And it's one of the primary reasons why both IT and business have to be committed to making digital work, and the reason why your digital agency may struggle to deliver a scaled digital project by themselves. It is very likely that your company's systems represent all the four challenges highlighted earlier. They are old and have been updated many times over, they represent a diverse set of suppliers and ages, and do not follow a standard interface model.

Yet, the way these applications interface and integrate to produce a usable service for your digital product or initiative is fundamentally critical to your success. This is why, middleware matters.

Middleware and Application Integration

As software systems have evolved sharply over the past couple of decades, there have been a number of different generations of application integration methods, tools, and concepts.

In lay terms, the starting point would be to simply couple any two applications that needed to talk to each other. Any application would typically have an application programming interface (API)—a way for another piece of software to ask it for information or to perform a task. The problem with this approach was that you couldn't replace either application without affecting the interface, so any change would cause a decline in service levels. Second, as you added more and more applications into the mix, your effort and costs would grow exponentially. In a typical enterprise, you could have up to 200 systems that need to communicate with each other—you can do the math on the challenge of point to point connects. This is why over time, more elegant approaches evolved.

A driving principle in software has in fact been to make it more Lego-like, through modular architectures. This means that even for a complex system, the individual components are clearly identifiable and are reasonably self-contained, with the goal being that you can take one module out and replace it with another similar component without breaking the overall system.

Along with the modularity, another key step is the evolution of service-oriented architecture (SOA). In this world, you design a system in a way that the software (or a software module) is represented as a series of services that can be defined, discovered, and transacted with, using some common and shared ways (including metadata). In the SOA world, you don't care if the backend system is a SAP or Oracle system. Or whether it sits on your premises or in the cloud. As long as another software (say a mobile application) can access the underlying services (e.g., tell me current inventory levels) through a well-defined interface, that's all that matters. This has therefore led to the creation of APIs that follow the framework and principles defined by SOA.

SOAP and ReST

You may hear both these terms while discussing APIs and middleware. Without going into technical details, what you need to remember is that both of these are different ways of writing APIs. Simple object access protocol (SOAP) is more robust, and would be used for online banking and transactions—where it's important for both parties to be able to confirm that a particular request went through and the transaction was recorded. Rest or representational state transfer (ReST) is a much more lightweight and more universal way of writing APIs and derives its advantage from the fact that the provider of the API and the consumer of the information know little about each other. Which works fine if you are a hotel website and you are consuming the Met Office's weather API. It's a loose relationship, the Met Office doesn't need to know whether or not you actually used that API.

Microservices

The drive toward granularity has led to the creation of micro-services that, as the name suggests, are much more finely grained service definitions.

These typically focus on just one task (or even what you might consider a subtask), and they are like smaller pieces of Lego you can combine differently. For example, a bit of code that just retotals the total in your shopping basket every time you make a change, adds tax and shipping, and calculates your net payment amount. The bits of software that add the tax and shipping are good potential examples of micro-services at work as well. Perhaps this figure is used in the shopping basket page but also as you continue to shop, this figure is displayed somewhere so the customer knows how much she is going to pay even as she continues to browse the virtual shelves.

API Management

As APIs proliferate, and boundaries of organizations become more and more porous, companies are finding themselves exchanging ever-higher amounts of information with external entities. If you work in a retail bank in Europe, for example, you are likely to be subject to the changes proposed by the PSD2 regulation,[1] which requires banks to provide customer data to any third party who the customer has selected, to aggregate their financial data (another bank, a fin-tech startup or a retailer that offers financial services). Besides, in the omnichannel world, your customer data has to be available across the Web, mobile, kiosk, store, and customer call center already. All of this points to an explosion in the need to serve information to an ever-growing set of systems and channels. This is where API management comes in.

In a nutshell, you will have a large number of APIs, which need to be managed with minimum cost, and with greatest impact and control. They need to confirm to standards of design, security, and maintainability. API management platforms allow you to manage and govern this set of APIs and prevent them from becoming a jungle of weeds. Through API platforms, you can control who gets to see and use which APIs and manage exceptions. APIs have become so common today that we often forget how different the structure of digital services was earlier. When the Amazon home page loads, it consumes up to 150 internal APIs, which are typically set up as micro-services.

Most companies now think of the API management as an enterprise-wide layer (nowadays sometimes referred to as an Integration Engine) to connect multiple apps and services to each other and to the backend systems. You should ideally plug into your organization's API management system, rather than create your own. If your service publishes APIs for other to use, you probably want a dashboard to track who is using them, how often, and for what purposes.

> Tip: Think about all the businesses that could to consume the service or information you offer, and imagine how they could integrate it into their customer offering.

The strategic role of API management can be seen in the way API management tools have been acquired by technology majors. Apigee was bought by Google, Mashery is now the Tibco Cloud API Management, and MuleSoft is now a part of Salesforce. In the ecosystem of businesses, APIs are the links between systems and information. Your taxi booking service works because it can consume a map API such as Google Maps, and tools like CityMapper work because they consume APIs from underlying transport systems in each city that they work in.

Consuming APIs

We have talked primarily about pushing out your own information as APIs so far, but you could be consuming external APIs for your product as well. In fact, you should actively scan the network for APIs, which you can be used to improve your service. If you are digitizing the customer experience for a golf course, you might start with location and weather APIs. Beyond this, you may find APIs from other golf sites, equipment makers, and magazines, which allow you to enrich your application, or social media APIs so that your customer can post her excellent score on her best friend's wall! If your user experience is critically dependent on an external API, it needs to be underpinned by a service contract, which covers areas such as change of terms, or service model, or even discontinuation of a particular API.

In Essence

As businesses become more networked, and the boundaries of organizations become more porous, we will collaborate and partner more voraciously in a networked environment, to create services that creatively combine functionality in real time. With the press of one button on your phone, you will trigger a series of events allowing you to check out of your hotel, summon an taxi, order a coffee at the coffee shop when you're nearing the airport, and check for flight departure gate information as it becomes available. To do all of these, we'll need APIs—the lubrication that allows the smooth ticking over of the digital universe.

CHAPTER 12

Digital Security

In the summer of 2021, in the middle of the pandemic response, while health care systems were already at the end of their tether, fighting the Coronavirus, a cyberattack took out the IT systems of the Health Service Executive (HSE), the public health care provider in Ireland. Projects were stopped, people had to use personal e-mails, and the inefficiency created no doubt cost lives, as the HSE was stretched to the limit. For example, a digital health project I was working on, which was already running behind owing to the pandemic, was further impacted by the cyberattack. The attack was reported to be carried out by a Russian criminal gang known as Wizard Spider. A number of patients' medical records were stolen and published online. The head of the HSE was quoted in the *Irish Times* as saying that the breach would cost the HSE €100m to fix.

There are millions of cyberattack attempts every week of the year. In the last few weeks of completing the editing and finalizing of this book, a software vulnerability surfaced on the Internet related to Log4j, a tool, that is used innocuously but almost ubiquitously on the Internet. In the first week of the discovery, over 1.2 million hacking attempts were made to exploit this vulnerability alone. Cyberattacks are mainstream events now, and no longer a source of surprise. Consider for example, the following picture, which shows a few significant cyberattacks across the year 2021. Not all breaches are as damaging as the HSE breach, but according to an IBM report, which surveyed 500 firms, the cost of data breaches on average has risen to $4.24m in 2021, which is higher than it's ever been before.

You might also recall that in 2015, a notorious Canadian business called Ashley Madison, which offered a platform for extramarital affairs, was hacked. The names of the customers, including some well-known people, were made public. It created an uproar and ripples across the world, ruining relationships and reputations. The bad news is that you

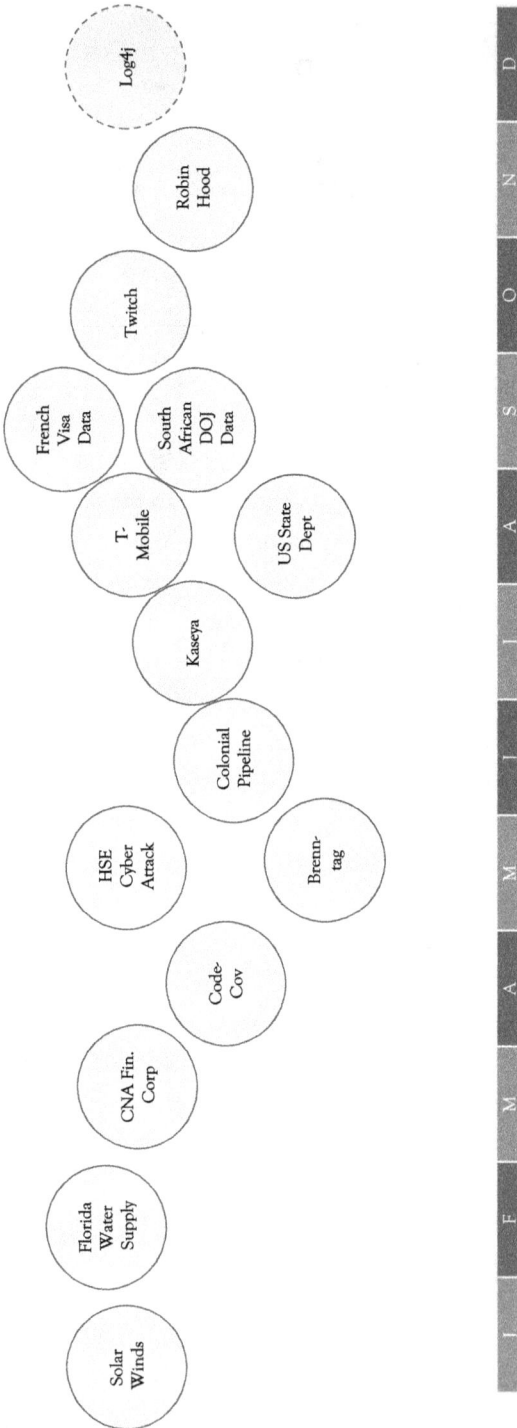

Figure 12.1 A sample of high-profile cyberattacks throughout the year 2021

Source: Data gathered from Arctic Wolf, Hackmageddon, Symantec, and other well-known websites.

don't have to be a business with a morally questionable premise, or reliant on the secrecy of your customers. No matter what your business, we are getting to a point in the digital era where the chances are information security breaches and cybercrime can bring your organization down to its knees. If in doubt, see *Home Depot*[1] or *Sony Pictures*[2] or *Experian*,[3] *Talk Talk*,[4] or sadly even *VTech Toys*.[5]

The bottom line is, every manager needs to get up to speed on cybersecurity.

Laxness about personal cybersecurity is probably something most of us are guilty of, surviving as we do with simple alphanumeric passwords that we share across banks, social media, and the random ecommerce site we signed up for last week. This piece isn't about personal security though, so we'll just leave it at that. But as we'll see, they're not entirely disconnected from each other.

In the past 18 months, almost every business has had to make a sharp turn toward digital, thanks to the pandemic. For a start, this has resulted in millions of people working from home, creating new *attack surfaces*. There's also a surge in ecommerce and online transactions. This is in addition to the underlying trend of digitization. Previously, you might have sold a thermostat or a blood sugar monitor. Increasingly, you're selling a connected version of these devices, with the date flowing back to your cloud-based setup, and a greater part of the value of your business is captured in the data, analytics, and insight, rather than the physical device. In this environment, the risks include your duty of care to protect customers and the regulatory requirement as a custodian of consumer data. And as an organization, your business and employee data are always your primary concern.

The motivation behind cyberattacks may be commercial or national. Cyberespionage is now an essential part of national and international intelligence. Many countries leave national fingerprints when it comes to cyberwarfare.[6] There's plenty of collateral damage involved here. You could be one of the companies targeted, for a host of reasons, or you could just fall prey to the future avatar of the Stuxnet. On the other hand, you could be a victim of a purely commercial criminal activity, where the miscreants are looking for commercial gain.

The purpose of a cyberattack could also be varied. Data theft is a common one, denial of service is another—also known as ransomware—as

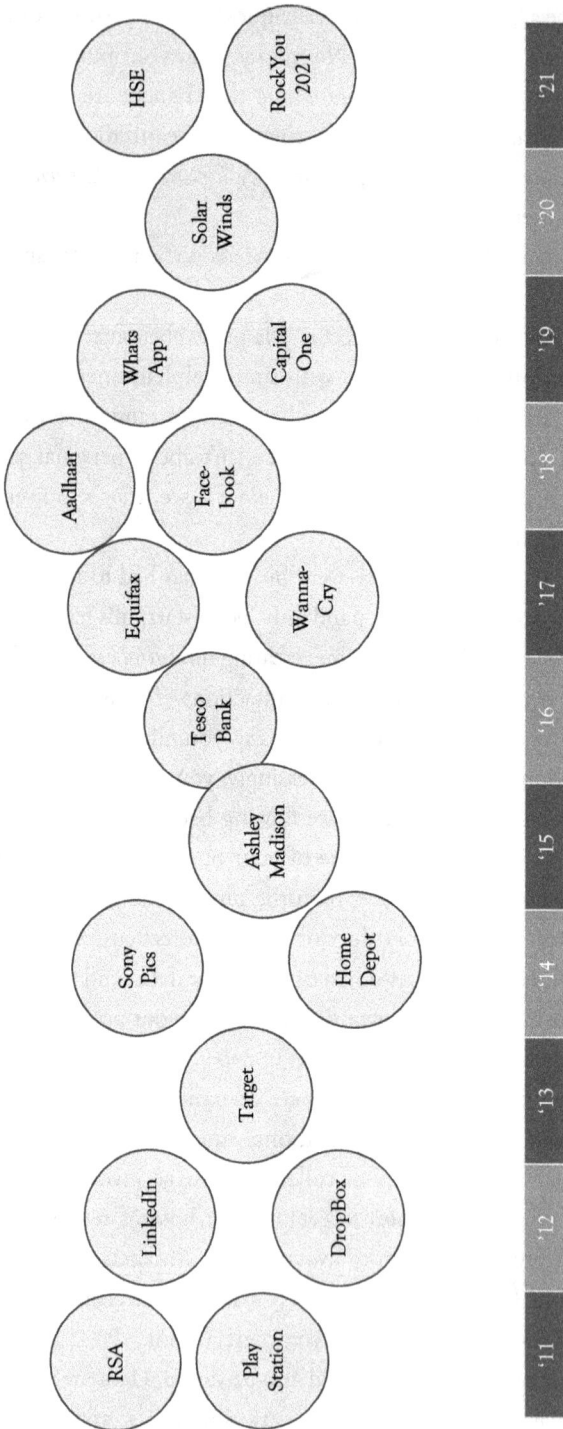

Figure 12.2 A sample of high-profile cyberattacks over the past decade

Source: Data gathered from Arctic Wolf, Hackmageddon, Symantec, and other well-known websites.

the hackers will usually ask for money in exchange for releasing code that will unlock your systems and allow you to use them again. For public-facing websites, a distributed denial of service (DDOS) can also be launched over the public Internet through botnets. Finally, there are also numerous variations in the method of cyberattacks. Compromised user credentials are the most common, as are vulnerabilities in off-the-shelf software, or human error by programmers or infrastructure managers. Enterprises are increasingly adopting a zero-trust model of cybersecurity—where every user has to demonstrate credentials before accessing confidential information, each time they do so.

The point is that this is a complex and multifaceted space, and you need to have a security risk management plan and monitoring. A simple version of this would display data on attempted cyberattacks, discovered security bugs, measures taken, and incidents reported. The actual execution of cybersafety measures should be left to the experts in your organization, but as a digital owner, you should ensure you understand and manage the risks. And needless to say, you need to bring in cybersecurity expertise in any digital project.

Privacy Versus Security

The security discussion also frequently overlaps with the privacy debate, and to make matters worse, privacy acts on both sides of the argument. On the one hand, a privacy loss is somewhat similar to a security breach—that is unauthorized people have access to your information. Yet, often privacy and security are seen as tradeoffs, as surveillance becomes a key tool against crime. Put that discussion to one side for now as well, and let's focus on the risk of cybersecurity.

Security Versus User Experience

A lot of work goes into a cybersecurity framework, from identify and authentication, to access control, encryption, and audit trails. However, one of the emergent themes over the past few months has been the role of user experience. All too often, excessive security measures kill the user experience of applications. When that happens, you get people bypassing security measures for no reason apart from avoiding irritation, but thereby creating potentially disastrous loopholes in your security environment. It's critical therefore that you focus on the user experience that your security regime imposes. A standard two-factor authentication system today uses the smartphone in conjunction with Web applications, with the addition of biometrics (fingerprint or face recognition on smartphones). This actually improves user experience by making the process faster.

Wanted: A Network View of Security

Another byproduct of digital business involves the blurring of boundaries. With more and more noncore functions outsourced, and businesses becoming leaner, the level of interconnects in businesses is going up manifold. Your supply *chain*, your distribution system, and your support ecosystem now resemble inter-dependent networks much more than chains. This introduces yet another dimension of risk, as much of your business information now flows through this network of partners. In 2015, Tien Phong Bank in Vietnam foiled a million-dollar cyber heist. The scammers sent fraudulent inter-bank transfer messages via the SWIFT system, which they accessed through a vendor's infrastructure. You will never be able to lock down every possible loophole, but conducting regular vendor audits on information security is certainly a good starting point. Major banks are already starting to conduct detailed supplier audits for information governance and security.

All of this collectively will not make you *safe*. Every innovation across technology and business will open up new security vulnerabilities. After all, as the world goes more digital with every passing day, we're opening up more opportunities for cyber harm and attacks. Hackers will get sophisticated. New tools and technologies such as AI and robotics will enter the fray. In fact, the biggest mistake one can make in this space is becoming complacent.

Tip: Talk to your organization's cybersecurity expert about your digital project. Also, list every possible way that somebody could access critical code or data in your system. Get others in your team to do the same.

The Cyber Security Arms Race

There is increasing sophistication on both sides of the cyberwar. Would-be attackers and cyberdefenders are able to deploy more sophisticated technology. This is progressing along three axes. The first is intelligence and software: AI tools cannot only look for hacking patterns and attempts at breaking in, they can also identify key stroke variations, time delay on password entry, and even unusual pressure applied to the keyboard compared to what is normal for you. Similarly, hackers are able to use and share tools that are able to spot vulnerability patterns in your systems. The second is hardware: quantum encryption is likely to take shape over the next decade, as quantum computing could break current complex alphanumeric passwords with ease. Third, the rise of biometrics: in the future, we may be identified by our *brainprints,* but voice, retina, fingerprint, and face recognition are all well under way. But let's not forget that any system is only as strong as its weakest link and people can be compromised as well. When it comes to cybersecurity, therefore, a healthy paranoia may be your best friend.

PART 3

Quantify

CHAPTER 13

Welcome to the Data Jungle

Every Question Ever Asked

Right now, as I write this, I'm thinking about some of the big and small decisions I have to make today. Should I add sugar to my coffee? Should I have a haircut before my meeting? Should I be reminding the firm I'm talking to about the job offer they are supposed to send me? Should I spend my time today finishing the proposal to prospective publishers about this book? At a granular level, every action we take personally or professionally involves data. In the examples I used, this could be data about calorie counts, who I'm meeting, what when I last spoke to the company in question, and so on. For almost all of these, the data we process is implicit, often even not a result of conscious thought. But we do decide to dry our hair when it's wet or turn into our gates when we reach our houses—I mean each of these is an active choice we make. Under the hood, we're constantly processing data, and often a lot of complex data as well—think of how much data you're actually processing while driving or cycling or even crossing the road on foot. Professionally, a lot of our decisions are more explicit, but all too often, the underlying reasoning and data are not. We rely our experience—which is nothing but an implicit and accumulated mental data-store, while making decisions on how long to set a meeting for, how often to write a blog or what should go into our calendar. Or even aspects of our hiring plan, business strategy, or sales presentation. We may not even be aware that we're processing years of accumulated data, but we are. Think of it this way: every question ever asked in the history of humankind is a request for data. And the only true purpose of data is to improve decision making. The fundamental challenge of data is therefore to connect the right data, at the right time, to decision points.

Has data has always been around? Shawn DuBravac points out in *Digital Destiny*[1]—*data was always present even before humans. We just didn't have a way of capturing and harnessing it.* This is a moot point, and I think we should distinguish between fact and data. Dinosaurs roaming the earth is a fact. But it only becomes data when this is recorded. Data therefore requires the human articulation of facts. Language therefore was critical to the creation and sharing of data. Writing allowed persistence, printing enabled mass distribution and digital technologies gave it superpowers.

Clive Humby was known for cocreating the data engine for Tesco's famously successful customer analysis, in Britain. But history will probably remember him more for coining the phrase "*data is the new oil*" in 2006. This has been quoted by strategists, architects, and CEOs across the world as the value of data became apparent over the past decade. Companies such as IBM and even Google, have built their entire business strategy around the value of data. But when it comes to your digital transformation, a good way to look at data is through the lens of quantification.

The last two years have been incredibly disruptive due to the global COVID-19 pandemic. But it has also been an education on the importance and centrality of data in our lives. Every day, for the past 20 months, we've been buffeted by pandemic-related news and information, and we've had to figure out how to read the insights behind the hysterical headlines and agenda-driven messages. A very good example came during the first deadly wave in Europe. While several countries were choosing to underestimate the actual number of fatalities by how they classified deaths during the pandemic, the *Economist* magazine carried data on *excess fatalities*— the gap between typical deaths in each country every year versus those reported this year. Depressing though this is, it provided a much clearer picture of what was really going on.

The Purpose of Data

Most ecommerce websites live and die by their data. If you're in the business of selling travel, or insurance, or secondhand cars via your website, and if you're reasonably successful, then it's likely that you have thousands, or even millions of people visiting your website every month. And for ecommerce, everything that happens on the website is a highly measurable funnel. The number of people who came to the site, the number of people who searched, the number that looked at a product, or how many products they looked at. How many added a product to the basket, and finally, how many checked out and paid. Most large ecommerce businesses track these numbers to the hour, or even minutes. The impact of any changes made to the site—even something as small as changing the color of the button is instantly visible as people either react positively or negatively (or sometimes not at all), and you know very quickly which it is.

The question is, why would you decide to change the color of any button, or change the way your shopping basket looks and behaves? Or even how your search works? Either you're shooting in the dark, or you have some idea of where the problem is. For example, if the industry average for shopping basket abandonment (the percentage of people who add items to a shopping cart but never check out) in your industry is 1 percent, but you're getting between 3 and 5 percent—this should tell you that something needs to be fixed. But you only know this if you've been tracking your data. Which is why, we come back to this double-edged value of data. It is both a trigger for your decision making and ideally, also a way to measure the impact of your decisions. In the digital world, you only get to this point if you have the initial *Connect* done well. Unless enough people are connecting with you via your site, your app, or your service, you won't even have the data to make these calls. In the traditional world as we'll see soon, we were only getting this data as an epilogue—well after the point when we could do something about it.

Operating in a VUCA World

There's also the matter of speed. You need the data when you're making the decision. And increasingly, you're having to make decisions in near-real time because the world is changing fast. The term VUCA captures this well. It stands for volatile, uncertain, complex, and ambiguous. Volatility means that the change is sudden. Uncertain means that it's not clear what direction it's taking. Complex means that the factors driving the change are unclear. And ambiguous means that we don't quite know what the status is at present. I'm sure that over the past two years, through the course of the pandemic, you've experienced each of these scenarios. Think of this—in 2019, the world leader in videoconferencing was Cisco, with its Polycom brand. In the consumer space and professional space, it would have been Skype. Over the next two years, videoconferencing went through the roof, with usage going up exponentially. Yet, neither Cisco nor Skype is leading the market today. It's largely Zoom and Teams that have captured the market. Skype and Teams are at least both part of Microsoft. But the way in which Zoom has left everybody behind in the personal calling space is telling, isn't it?

In this VUCA world, you're constantly on the frontline and having to make tactical or strategic calls. This is the reason why your data is so critical. And why mature ecommerce firms are so focused on the data from every step of their customers' journey.

The pandemic is an appropriate example of the VUCA environment, where companies—especially in travel and hospitality—have had to create dashboards that track the impact of COVID-19 on their daily operations. Locations that are open or closed, areas where employees and customers need to take special precautions, and so on. As I write this, the omicron variant is causing more consternation and additional constraints on travel. From day to day, we need to know which countries, cities, or regions are impacted, where governments are likely to impose lockdowns or restrictions, and where the risks too our employees and customers are beyond the acceptable threshold, and act accordingly, in near-real time.

The irony is that even as we look for the right data for our decision making, we're in the middle of a data flood. The amount of data we have access to is many orders of magnitude more than before. Let's take a closer look at this tsunami of data.

Industry 4.0—The Era of Abundance

Around the end of 2021, atop the mountains in the Elqui province of Chile, a new observatory is being completed, with the world's largest ever digital camera. Actually, it's more than a camera, it's a telescope. To get an idea of its size, consider that the mirror is 27 feet in diameter, and the lens was created out of 22 tons of molten glass. It has 32 giga pixels of resolution (that's 32,000 megapixels). The telescope will point out at the sky and retrieve images every 15 seconds, armed with over 200 sensors, will generate 6 million gigabytes of data every year. Which is the roughly the same amount of data you would generate if you took half a million pictures with your new iPhone 13 with its 12-megapixel camera every night for a year.

And yet, probably the most salient aspect of this mass of data is that it doesn't feel particularly newsworthy. There is a data explosion all around us that is the result of the explosion in connections. A lot of what used to be analog and human-driven now is increasingly driven through devices and systems. This includes, for example, taking pictures, paying money, booking taxis, connecting with friends and colleagues, reading books and magazines, or even the number of steps we—all of which we now do through our smartphones. At work, this includes e-mails, accessing files and customer information, filling time sheets and expense reports, and thanks to the pandemic, even attending meetings. Even at an environmental level—the weather, traffic conditions, and even pollen count are now monitored via smart and connected sensors. As we've seen in the chapters earlier, everything, including our own bodies and brains, are becoming sources for new data streams. As all these digital connections create giant flows of data, it's up to us whether to tap into this. We are in the middle of a transition from *implicit to explicit* data in our decision-making models. One of the immediate benefits of this should be that we are able to make better and more informed decisions, but there's an interim step required—we need to build the skills and knowledge required to manage all this data.

Arguably, this flood of data has changed the rules for how businesses compete. Along with storage and computing power, data is plentiful and accessible at low costs. We now operate in an era of abundance. This is decidedly different from the economic basis of the past centuries, where we were largely competing for scarce resources. Abundance requires a different mindset—where the focus has to be on identifying the most valuable parts of a nearly infinite resource. Some call this the Industry 4.0 model. Whatever the framework you use, and whichever industry you're in, there's little doubt that we find ourselves today sailing in an ocean of data.

Managing the Data Deluge

You see articles every other day talking about how Data Science is the hottest job in the 21st century. By now you've probably gotten sick of hearing about big data, little data, fat data, thin data, and all manner of data. But this is the core, the engine. The successful firm of the future will have a data-driven engine room. It's important that we get our heads around terabytes, exabytes, and zettabytes, and the changing economics of data. In 1986, the world's total data storage capacity was 2.6 exabytes. An exabyte is a billion gigabytes. In 2005, just under 20 years, that was 295 exabytes. In 2013, we created 4.4 zettabytes of data (a zettabyte is a 1,000 exabytes), and by 2020, the volume of data rose to 64.2 zetta-bytes. Here's a sample of what happened on the Internet on average in every minute in 2020, according to DOMO who publishes this annu-ally—over 41 million WhatsApp messages were shared, 200,000 Zoom meetings were held, 400,000 hours of Netflix shows were downloaded, almost 70,000 users applied for jobs on LinkedIn, and Amazon shipped over 6500 packages. *In every minute.*

This tsunami of data has created its own challenge of data manage-ment—creating products from Hadoop and MongoDB to data lakes and data puddles, which we'll talk about later. The scary part of all of this is that we're still in the relatively early days of the data deluge. We are hurtling into a quantified universe fed by smart cities, homes, and cars; platform-driven models and clickstream-driven relationships. Ultimately, data is the end-game of digital transformation.

This data deluge is complex not only because of its sheer size, but as we've highlighted already—the speed at which it is being collected, and the sophistication of the interrelationships between the data—all of these require the creation of a whole new data management toolkit. Four distinct developments have changed the way we manage and consume this big data: the cost of storage, the design of databases, the cost of band-width, and the improvement in retrieval technologies.

Tip: Think about the total volume of data in your business. Now mul-tiply that by 10, and assume that all that data is coming into your business in real time. That is what you'll probably have to deal with within the next five years.

CHAPTER 14

Data in the Enterprise

Flood and Famine: Rethinking Enterprise Data

For many large companies, there's no shortage of data in the business. You probably have sales data, customer information, supply chain data, and a vast number of additional sets of data. This can often lull managers into believing that they've got enough data. But the right way to think about this is through the lens of your decisions. If you're looking to improve your product performance, how much data do you have about how customers are using your product. Or if you're rationalizing your store locations, are you doing this with the data you need? Is there a mismatch between the data you have and the decisions you need to make? Do you find yourself in situations where you have some but not all the data you need? Does it take too long to get the data in a usable form? Are you having to custom create reports that require days and weeks to get done? These are all the typical problems I've seen in organizations that also simultaneously feel that they have more data than they're actually using. It is definitely possible for both of these to be true. You have data sets A, B, C, and D. You need data sets C, D, E, and F. Your data team is complaining that you don't use all the data you already have, and you feel you're not getting the data you need.

> Tip: Take any decision you need to make at work and think of all the information that you would need to make a perfect decision. Then see what percentage of information is available to you.

Analytics and Business Intelligence

The idea that by capturing data about business operations, we might find ways to improve them goes back to the start of the 20th century, to the time of Henry Ford and Frederick Taylor. Since then, and especially spurred on by computerization, spreadsheets, and many more sophisticated tools, most businesses use analytics and business intelligence or BI extensively. Walmart was famous for leading the charge on gathering and exploiting retail data not just for its own operations but also for sharing with all its providers and partners.

It's a useful practice, while embarking on any digital project, to envision the postproject state, and think about what data you will be generating, how you want that data to be presented, and what decisions you want to be making with that data. Each of these questions might impact the other, but working back from this will shape your project much more effectively. Otherwise, you will end up with a lot of data being thrown into a generic dashboard that nobody actually uses. Most data now lives in the cloud, and it makes sense that the analytics and BI tools are also similarly on the cloud—a good example is Splunk, a tool that captures data across your IT environment, and provides data, tools, and reports in the cloud. This means that the entire process can run where the data is, and what gets delivered is the specific report or data stream that you need. For example, if you're digitizing a call center, with online human chats and chatbots, once the project is complete, every customer conversation will generate data. You'll be able to run sentiment analysis, keyword analyses, and more. You might also get geographical information and device information, which is additionally useful to your marketing team. You could then provide a bunch of report options and allow the business managers to create their own parameters to choose from, for reporting. The training manager could look at the escalations and average time per conversation. The chatbot design team could look at levels of engagement and handover. The head of customer service could look at the average time to resolution and satisfaction levels. Each of these people could run their own reports, choose the period of reporting, and add and remove parameters (split by age of user, or type of customer, etc.). You've now reached the stage of providing the reporting *as a self-service* option.

You would then typically add visualization tools. There's a longer discussion a little later, but for now, let's remember that there's already a huge push for visualization and *infographics*. The latter often turns into throwing pictures and words together. But the purpose of both are the same—to use the best possible means to communicate complex information in a way that's easy to absorb and memorable.

> Tip: Resist the urge to add unnecessary embellishments in your data visualization, especially if the user has to see the same report regularly.

Collectively, these data analytics tools are referred to as systems of insight, for obvious reasons. It's worth noting that multiple types of analytics works coexist within these environments. Not everything is required at the same velocity and urgency, so costs can be traded off. Some data is inherently structured, such as customer names and contacts, while others such as weather or relationship information, or the spread of disease or crime, is inherently unstructured. Appropriate tools and methodologies are required for each.

Avoiding Data Antiquity

One day, just a few years ago, I lost my debit card. I say lost, but my daughter, then four, discovered it under the car seat the next day. By then, I had canceled the card via the bank website, and my bank assured me that a new one was on its way. As it turned out, this was within a day of my wife's card expiring, so she was also talking with the same bank for the same purpose—a new debit card.

A week went by and no cards showed up, so we started following up. Imagine our surprise when we were told that the card had been dispatched, but to our previous address—which we had left exactly 13 months earlier. The bank didn't know that we had moved. How was this possible? Even worse, they had my old mobile phone number—which I had not used in 6 months.

Having moved home a few times, we have a comprehensive checklist for all services we need to update. From utility providers, to post office, to banks to employers, it's all there, and we're pretty sure we did it all. In fact, our credit cards, with the same bank had all the right information. We received the statements, and our online purchases went through with the new address confirmation. But, this information had not filtered through to the savings account side of my bank.

And consider this: quite apart from the inconvenience and the confusion, the bank had effectively posted my card *and* my pin to the wrong person. It was sent by registered post—but as we know, anybody can really sign for it. How ironic is it that after all the effort of sending the card and pin in separate packs and taking all the precautions of masking the pin, it gets sent to the wrong person! A reminder that you're only as secure as your weakest link!

You're probably thinking at this point that the credit card business and the consumer banking business may not be sharing data. But even without sharing data, it's easy to highlight it when address data for the same customer is different across the parts of the business, or flag it to the other business one when one address has changed. The alternative, as in this case, was to put the onus back on the consumer to notify each individual branch of the bank individually, about change of address. That can't be right. I'm sure you've had similar experiences with either your bank or your health care provider, utility provider, or some other service you consume. And I'm sure many of you, like me, have been unwilling recipients of retargeting ads—being told about great new folding cycles a month after you searched for and bought it. How many such businesses are trying to leap into the 21st century, with one foot still stuck in the 1980s?

Real-Time Data

If data is at the heart of decisions, then data systems are effectively the nervous system of the organization. The ability of a business to react to its environment depends critically on its ability to bring the relevant data to its decision points, at the right time. The art and science of managing data in the organization is one of the most critical skills for digital organizations today. This is an area that has gone through huge changes in the digital era.

For a lot of businesses, even 10 years ago, it took a while for businesses to even understand their own performance. Broadcast businesses, for example, were dependent on data produced by the Broadcasters' Audience Research Bureau or the BARB in the UK. BARB collects viewership data based on a sample and reports back to the broadcasters. It used to be a two-week cycle and is now an overnight one. At some point, this will be near-real time, or the broadcasters will know within minutes if not seconds of airing a show how many people watched it, or perhaps they will know the figures even as the show is airing. The competition from traditional TV channels is no longer other TV channels but online video. Be it Netflix, Prime, Disney+, YouTube, or any other. And any over-the-top (OTT) provider, as they are called, because they bypass the broadcast infrastructure, knows what their audience is watching every minute, in real time. They know when you paused your show and when you skipped the credits. And what you searched for and browsed before you selected something to watch. When Prime broadcasts sports, as they now do, they also know if you switched off during the game, or if you rewound a part of the action.

Today, a lot of businesses have moved to real-time data. Tools such as SAP HANA enable the aggregation and analysis of data in real time, that is, as it happens. An apparel retail chain may want to know its daily sales and stock figures an hour after stores close, in a region, or the relative performance of different colors within a line, in order to move stock for the next day or place new orders on suppliers. The faster movement of data has enabled faster business cycles. Zara and H&M were brands that built competitiveness around the speed of their business cycles. Traditional shoppers visited apparel stores four times a year, but Zara customers came in once every three weeks for new fashions. But now they have been superseded by the next generation such as BooHoo and Asos who are running at *Internet speed.* Zara was revolutionary for offering hundreds of new items a week; nowadays, Asos adds as many as 7,000 new styles to its website over the same period.

The New Crystal Ball: Predictive Data

We aren't stopping at the present. Future telling may have been a black art with crystal balls in fair grounds, but today, a lot of near-future outcomes are predictable, given the patterns, with a high degree of accuracy.

DeepMind, an Alphabet company, works with the Royal Free Hospital Trust in London to help predict acute kidney infections, thereby saving lives saving as saving nurses two hours per day on average. This is just one example, you only have to read the newspapers to see everyday instances of predictive date analysis in managing customer churn, or in managing maintenance work on asset networks. Over the next few years, we will see the focus of AI in any number of ways looking to predict the near future.

Knowledge Management 2.0

There have been multiple points over the past 40 years when the term *knowledge management* was in vogue. As the Internet was spreading its wings across commerce, content, and supply chains, it suddenly became apparent that we were sitting on one of the largest treasure troves of information ever, and it was accessible to everybody. Knowledge management involved the idea that we could get our experts to share their knowledge and experience through systems, which would allow this knowledge to be passed on to others. The support engineer who has been fixing gas leaks for 20 years would share the patterns, experiences, and challenges in a way that the novice engineer could access and gain from. Or an experienced nurse could contribute to building an expert system that could run basic diagnostics for a person with basic symptoms. Every major company was looking to recast their products as knowledge management systems—from IBM's Lotus, to Microsoft Collaboration tools, to Oracle Databases. It never took off. Not because the technology was missing, but the assumption that experts would have the incentives and the time and even the capability to articulate their methods, data, and experience in a structured manner was a flawed one in the main. The power of *gut* decisions is also their weakness. They are near impossible to replicate.

Today, we might be reaching the same point but through a very different route. By connecting all these experts to systems that enable them to do their job better, we are getting them to create that same dataset of their choices, and experiences, almost as a byproduct. By getting a service engineer to log a job on a phone or scan a barcode to identify a part, we gather not just the core data about which customer, what job, which spare part, and what problem, but also meta-data—time, location, duration between jobs, etc., which collectively give us a richer data set to work with. Over time, this would give us the same kind of *knowledge* capability that we were seeking back then, but without trying to get people to simply dump their knowledge into an artificial system.

Adding Love to Data

A few years ago, at the annual FT Innovate Conference, a lively round-table discussion followed after a well-known retail CEO had made a presentation about data and analysis. The presentation covered examples of analyzing customers to great and occasionally worrying insight, within the industry. From knowing if a woman is pregnant even before she knows it herself, to people having affairs, or stacking beer and nappies together, in front of the stores, all of this can today be deduced from data itself.

Let's remind ourselves though—while there's been a lot of talk about analyzing customers, it misses the point of empathy. The customer does not want to be analyzed. As with any relationship, he or she wants to be loved, cherished, understood, and served better. At the end of the day, for most businesses, this translates to a mind-shift again, of adding a layer of human understanding to data, to creatively and emotionally assess the customers' needs, and to allow the analytics to feed off the empathy and emotional connect, rather than be driven purely by the algorithm.

Data Visualization

Imagine that you're trying to control a cholera epidemic in the 19th century. Although everybody believes that the disease is airborne, you have a hunch that it might be something else. You gather data about cholera patients and you have their names, ages, and addresses. If you're John Snow, the famous physician, you plot the cases on a map, overlay it with the visual of the water supply and sewage, and establish your hypothesis that the spread of the disease follows the water system, rather than over the air. Look at the following picture, which shows the cholera-impacted households in Soho, London. Now just for a moment, imagine that instead of this map, you have a table with names and addresses, and you have another table describing the path of sewage systems. Do you think

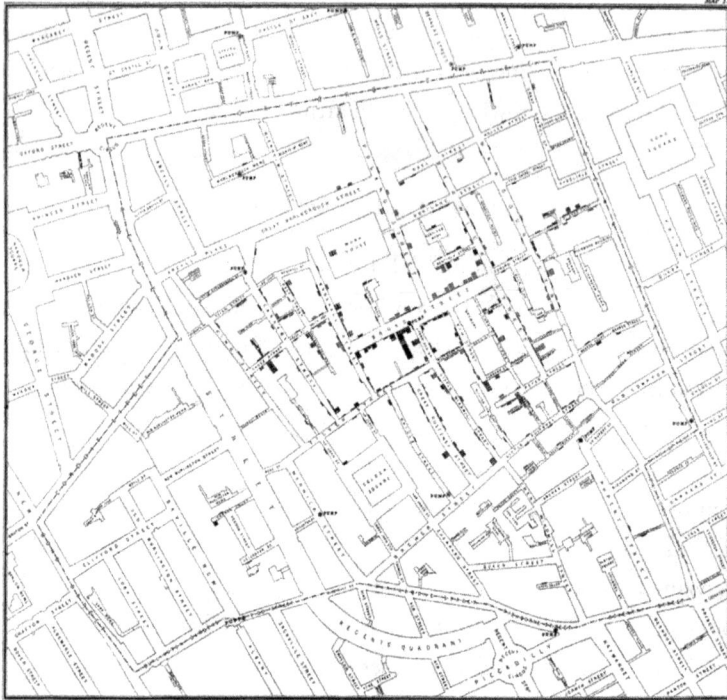

Figure 14.1 Cholera/sewage map—John Snow

it would be as easy to assess the linkage between the disease and the water system? Sure, it could be done, but it would hardly be as intuitive as when you look at the map. John Snow not only established the cause of spread of cholera, he's credited with being a pioneer of epidemiology—the science of tracking epidemic diseases.

You can look at data in any way you want, but there's obvious merit to presenting it in a way that will aid decision making. This can work in two ways. Either we know the needs of the decision, and the data is presented accordingly. Or we use the data to trigger new thoughts for decision makers. For example, the decision of "where to open our next store" will involve a lot of geographic data—including customer clusters, competition, and potentially complementary products. All of this will make more sense visually on a map. On the other hand, data from a patient's health wearable showing level of movement might be best presented using a 360° clock interface. Getting too creative with data is a risk if it gets in the way of decision making, or if it masks the decision data. A good visualization uses every aspect of the visual—color, shape, size, position, and relationship, to draw focus on the key decision criteria, and tries to keep it as simple as possible. As a simple example, tools like Microsoft Word, or Gmail, which people use frequently, have to be extremely understated, so as not to get on your nerves over time. The designers have to strongly resist the urge for unnecessary flourishes. This is also true of data visualization—so be clear about whether it's a single-use visualization or something that will be used frequently. There are a number of tools for visualization, the most popular ones in corporations tend to be Tableau, Qlik, and Microstrategy, but open-source tools such as Charted have gained ground as well.

Data Economics—The Crown Jewels

Adrian Slywotzky's great book on *Value Migration*[1] talks about how economic value migrates from older to newer business models or from a segment to another, or even one firm to another. In the digital era, we are going to see significant value moving to those companies in each industry that get the value of the data, be it health care, or education, or automobiles, insurance, or even heavy industry. The Howden Group of companies (formerly Hyperion) has been known for underwriting and brokerage in the European insurance space. Hyperion X is the business within the portfolio that offers data insights to other insurers and brokers. This is just one example of many businesses looking to trade off the value of their data capabilities.

It's the reason why Google bought Nest for a valuation far higher than any thermostat company could hope to get, or why startups such as 23AndMe are valued at $3.5 billion—you can see the data-centric companies starting to become value magnets. The question you want to be asking yourself is, in your industry and in your firm, what are some of the areas of opportunity where you can create new platforms to data-enable processes, or value to customers. How can you converge the primary and ancillary meaning in your data onto areas of your competitive strategy? And also, you may want to perform an audit of what data you might be giving away, perhaps because you feel that it's not core to your business or you have a player in the industry who has historically been collecting this data. For example, Experian and credit scores. Ask yourself, are you merely giving away data that you don't use, or are you handing over the source of competitive differentiation in your industry?

To underscore the earlier point, I believe that value will increasingly migrate, in each industry, to those who best manage, and build strategic and competitive alignment with their data strategies and/or new offerings based on the data and its meaning, while building trust and reducing friction.

> Tip: Identify the analog products, services, and processes in your business and try and explore the value of the data if these were digital processes.

Alongside the explosion of value data is the reduction in the unit cost of storage. In 1985, there weren't too many gigabyte storage options. But a 26 MB drive cost $5,000, which meant you were paying $193,000 per GB. In 1990, the price per GB had dropped to $105,000. In 1995, it was $11,000; in 2000, it dropped to $1,100; and in 2015, it was $0.05. In 2021, on Amazon's lowest pricing tier, you can get a GB of storage at $0.0125 Do you know anything else that went from a price of $193,000 to $0.0125 in 36 years? You can see why this reduction in storage costs is essential to and possibly an outcome of the explosion of data generation. This goes hand in hand with similar, if not same, reductions in the cost of bandwidth and computing.

CHAPTER 15

Data Architectures

Why Architecture?

The challenge of this approach is our ability to handle all the data we are now generating. In 2008, I spoke with a division of Autonomy (now HP) that had a product aimed at broadcasters. This system could ingest a video, strip out the audio file, convert it into text, and put it back together so that you could now search the video for any word spoken. It also converted any words it could find on the screen and used OCR (optical character recognition) to convert them to text, so a sign, a hoarding, or billboard could be similarly searched for. The system also ran a face recognition tool, so if the video included Bruce Springsteen, it could recognize Springsteen's face and make this a searchable field as well. In the nascent world of Web video, this could be really powerful as it would allow both end users as well as production and edit teams to search for any content by person, word, or text on screen. The product ran into one problem. The cost of storing and managing that data set almost doubled the cost of storing the video itself. At a time when broadcasters were still figuring out the cost of video storage, they simply didn't have the tools or budget for such a voluminous data set.

This is the problem that I lightheartedly call the unbearable bigness of data! We have so much data today that it hurts. We have terabyte drives sitting by our laptops sucking up our thousands of digital photographs and videos. We consume gigabytes of videos every day on Facebook or YouTube, on our mobile devices, without even thinking. Every act of ours leaves a digital data trail—a digital exhaust, which can be gathered and used by our service providers. We are plugged into global networks of social connections, smart energy, financial transactions, and in the foreseeable future, autonomous transport—zipping petabytes of data across the world. Even our bodies—now being understood at a subcellular and genome level—are generating data that is harvestable. Not only is this data insanely huge, it is also relatively unstructured. The challenge of dealing with this ever growing and unstructured data is what the industry calls *Big Data*.

Database Structures

For the longest time, the dominant way of storing data was in rows and columns in relational databases. Relational database management systems (or RDBMSs as they were called) stacked data in rows with an index. For example, a customer list in a CRM (customer relationship management) database would have customer name as a key but could have an address, contacts, and status as a columns. A separate table could have information on the 10 different kinds of statuses and what they meant; a third table could carry links between customers—such as family members. When these were indexed, searching became easy, for example, for a customer called John Smith or Raj Sen—you just had to index on the last name (i.e. sort by that column) and you wouldn't have to check each column but go straight to S and the name would either be in the right place or not at all, in the database. However, if you were searching for John or Raj—you would need to re-sort this by first names. You can see why this would be tricky if there were too many sort fields. Other reasons why RDBMSs were struggling to keep up with the digital data were the size of the data, the speed at which they were being added, and also, the lack of structure. If the data didn't have a clear rows and columns structure or the inter-relationships were too complex, this would be a problem. In the world of store transactions or clearly defined product catalogs, this wasn't a problem. But if you're trying to build a comprehensive view of the customer, as MetLife was looking to do in 2013, the relational database is no longer the right tool. When that view of the customer requires information about 100 products, sourced from 70 different systems, and you want to do that for 100 million customers—it needs a different kind of approach.

Hadoop/Spark

Today's applications solve these problems of volume, velocity, and variety of data using a number of new tools for data. You will definitely have heard of Hadoop if you've worked on any digital project with a lot of data over the past few years. Hadoop is actually just a file management software—analogous to your windows file system, but designed to handle huge amounts of data, which may not have a clear structure. Hadoop is structured for scale in a way that the data can be distributed across multiple clusters of servers and therefore scale more easily. Each bit of data is also stored in more than one server, so it's also more resilient—if one server goes down, the data is still accessible. Retrieval is done through a process called Map-Reduce. This method is a more efficient way of storing very large volumes of data, which may not be structured or may include documents tweets or multimedia files. In recent years, Hadoop has been superseded by Apache Spark, which, like Hadoop, is an open-source project. But Spark runs in memory, so is faster and much more suited to real-time search and retrieval, as well as real-time interactions, although the cost of RAM is higher. Another tool you might come across is Kafka, which is typically used alongside Hadoop or Spark, to handle streams and distributed messaging—say from a social media environment. Other tools from the Apache family include Hive (data warehousing), Flink (real-time event processing), and Storm (similar to Hadoop but works in real time rather than batches).

NoSQL

NoSQL is a database structure that uses *key value pairs* rather than rows and columns. This is a useful structure when not every item has the same descriptors. For example, a in a database of zoo animals, a key may be *wings,* and the value may be *red*, but not every animal will have them. Other keys could be *scales* or *horns*. This is more efficient than a row and column format with lots of blanks. MongoDB is one of the most popular NoSQL databases—and it was the tool used by MetLife in the preceding example, to build its single view of the customer.[1] Bear in mind that this approach isn't necessarily better in every way—you would probably still use RDBMS tools for handling transactions, or a traditional inventory management application. Hadoop/NoSQL isn't the best system for real-time retrieval of information and real-time processing, in the way you need for transactions.

Graph Databases

Another evolution that stems from the exponential growth of the inter-relationships between the data is Graph databases, which are a specific type of NoSQL databases. Graph databases are able to capture this complexity of inter-relationships, which would be incredibly difficult to map, manage, and maintain in a traditional RDBMS. For example, when a bank tries to evaluate a customer's credit risk based on their social network, or when you want to analyze the risk of fraud—you need to model a very high number of interconnected variables. As you can imagine, the social network of an individual is a complex network that is frequently changing—growing, shrinking, or shape-shifting, with clusters forming and dissipating over time. This is the home-turf of graph databases, which captures nodes and relationships in the data. In the case of fraud analysis, you may regularly encounter new information that doesn't fit your current data model. This too is another difference, as pointed out by Neo4J, a well-known provider of Graph Databases: in a traditional RDBMS database, you have to build the model before adding data—that is construct a row/column structure with column labels, and specify its relationship to the other rows and columns, before you can put in a row of new data. Yet, the specific challenge you face may well be a discovery driven one, as is likely with fraud analysis, so your model may evolve as your analysis progresses.

It's not just these obvious scenarios though, you can often reimagine current processes such as sales and customer service using a network model, as Telenor did with its approval process for new customers, to reduce response times from *minutes to milliseconds*. This network approach with inherently encoded nodes and relationships can be supported by graph databases, better than other formats.

The bottom line is that today, you don't need a one-size-fits-all approach to manage your data challenges. Instead, this should be a portfolio of options, each one with its specific advantages, and benefits, for the different kinds of problems it solves most efficiently. Also, any data strategy has to focus on the efficiency and effectiveness of storing data but also its retrieval. Data is useless if it can't be retrieved. So, while designing any data solution, you also need to be clear about the search and retrieval tools and strategy. For instance, Elastic Search, which is a tool designed for distributed document and data searches and often used on conjunction with Hadoop/NoSQL data.

Data Lakes

A lot of companies have moved to a model of data lakes because of the complexity of the data processing requirements. The data lake model holds data in *flat files*, rather than the rows and columns structure. The data lake stores the data in its native or original format until it is needed. So rather than apply a lot of resource-intensive cleaning, modeling, and processing, this is done in near-real time when the data is actually needed. Note that creating a data lake is not an outcome. It's the equivalent of creating the foundation of a building, or perhaps organizing the shelves in a retail store. The value is only delivered with the data is consumed.

Data Processes

For all this data to be usable, it needs to be prepared, processed, and modeled. Traditionally, businesses separated their data to keep transaction and reporting requirements separate. Databases designed for transactions were not best suited for reporting and vice versa. This hasn't really changed, as you can see. What has changed is that the analytical databases have become much more specialized and more innovative technologies have been used here to handle speed, volume, and inter-relationships. On the other hand, you still have the problem of data cleansing as a lot of data (especially from sources such as social media) may be incomplete and sometimes contain errors or duplication. This needs to be cleaned before it can be modeled.

CHAPTER 16

Data Evolution

What Before Why

A question I often ask my colleagues who are experts in data science is based on the hypothetical situation as follows: let's suppose that when it rains, people drink more cappuccinos. Now, if a coffee shop knew this, it could advertise or promote cappuccinos every time it rained. It could even launch branded umbrellas as a themed promotion. But how would it discover this? Historically, the story would be one of a smart store manager who one day realizes that rainy days increases his cappuccino sales, and having defined the premise, starts to collect the data to validate his hypothesis. Or even more traditionally, a major coffee shop brand runs focused groups, and the link between weather and coffee preferences is established. A qualitative hypothesis would be at the front of the process, and data collection would follow. Because, how else would we know if it's the rainfall or the pollen count or, indeed, the volume of traffic on the roads that we should be correlating coffee sales with?

In the new world of data, or *big data*, this works the other way around. The same coffee shop brand might take all their sales data across the world, and run hundreds or thousands of analyses, searching for correlation, with any number of external and easily accessible data sources. This includes the obvious ones such as weather, or transport, but also, for example, days of week or month, time of day, and train and bus schedules, sales in other retail stores, and so on. This list is only limited by your creativity and the data availability.

Think about this though, this is a shift from why to what. In this new world, we find the correlation first and then the hypothesis. And we may arguably not care why. Let's suppose we discovered that the coffee consumption varied with the tides. We would need to verify whether this was simply a spurious correlation, but once we established that the correlation was genuine, we could go straight to predictability and put to one side the logic, or the *why* question. This is a mind shift for those of us who are used to a *scientific* mentality, which requires us to establish scientific reasoning for any approach to rise beyond heuristics into a scaled and logical argument. I should highlight that this is a contestable perspective, and different viewpoints may exist. But as a manager, you may want to explore using the correlation, while as a scientist, you may be more concerned with understanding it better.

Data Ethics: With Regulation on Our Side

In 2016, the EU announced the General Data Protection Regulation (GDPR)—which is the effectively Data Protection Act (DPA) 2.0. Under the revised regulation, fines for violation go from half a million to 20 million pounds (or 4 percent of global turnover). And the requirements for auditable process and governance are much more onerous. In addition, consumers can make subject access requests (SARs) for their data, which companies must provide at no cost. Suffice it to say, my bank would not have passed this test! To address this problem, a key initial step is to conduct a data audit—to establish what personally identifiable information (PII) you may be holding anywhere within your business. But while the traditional approach to audit involves consultants with clipboards, a more digital process can be used. There are data discovery tools that use machine learning to address audit problem. Immediately, this becomes a connected and quantifiable way of looking at the near-real-time data map of the organization.

Data-Centric Organizations

You may by now have come to the same conclusion that I have, which is that most organizations need put data at the heart of their business. There aren't too many examples of this in sight, apart from the usual suspects—Google, Amazon, and Netflix. Many organizations still have a relatively small BI or analytics team whose job is to turn out *Management Information* reports that are predefined. These are usually understaffed and work on traditional BI tools, and on a subset of the data coming into the business, creating reports that typically report on the past.

As a first step, analytics and data need to be made a part of processes, as a matter of routine. A typical process of approving customers for a loan—needs to be enriched with new data, new models, and improved decisions support. But also processes that traditionally aren't as data driven need to be brought into the fold. Nicolaus Henkey, formerly of Quantum Black, and head of McKinsey Analytics, cites the example of a retailer looking to expand footprint in a city but struggling to find where they could expand their stores. The team deduced from a large data set that stores next to laundromats were doing very well. Using this discovery, they found 850 laundromat locations that could be used for new stores.

A lot of senior decision makers and business leaders have always used their experience and intuition and now have to lead the charge to a data-driven world. Culturally, this can be challenging, especially when the data suggests a counterintuitive answer. But when the data throws up something outside of the expected, this is where new opportunities and answers might lie, as evidenced by the preceding retail example.

Marketplaces

Here's an interesting question. What percentage of the data you consume at work every day originates outside of your organization? The chances are it's a significant amount, comprising a combination of your custom-ers' data, vendor data, data from your environment, and of course some of your original data as well. Yet, most of the effort and focus is on enterprise data.

How do we improve the way data moves between organizations? To start with, there are three typical features of how businesses exchange data. Think about the data exchange between a supermarket and a major con-sumer goods brand, or even an automotive OEM (Original equipment manufacturer) and a tire manufacturer. First, there's usually an existing commercial contract underpinning the relationship. The data sharing supports the existing relationship of goods and services exchange. Second, this is usually a bilateral arrangement—both the contract and the data exchange. And third, the data is clearly known and defined. For example, product or service specifications, stock position, or invoices, orders, rate cards, and so on. But what if none of these three conditions applied?

A perfectly good scenario to consider is Scope 3 Emissions reporting, in the sustainability space. For Scope 3, every organization has to be able to report on its upstream and downstream activities, which would mean vendors and clients. Just think about this for a second, GSK has 36,000 suppliers according to their annual report. Sainsburys, the retailer, has over 2,000 suppliers. All of these suppliers have to provide their emissions data to customers such as GSK and Sainsburys. In fact, quite a few suppliers may be common to GSK and Sainsburys—technology providers, telecom providers, and many others. We therefore have a many-to-many scenario, rather than a bilateral model. No agreement to share this data currently exists. Which means that the rules or constraints governing sharing or consuming of this data haven't been defined yet. And finally, we don't even know at present which data will be relevant in future. And whether new regulations, technologies, or data sets will emerge and change the landscape. You can see why the traditional approach of defined, contracted, and bilateral data exchange doesn't work here.

What these kinds of environments need are *data marketplaces*. A marketplace has the ability to support discovery, description, negotiation, contract, and transfer of the commodity—in this case, data. The marketplace supports the scenario where you don't necessarily know exactly what you're looking for. To take a trivial example, imagine that you're cooking dinner for friends and you have a menu in mind. You could just go to a website and order the specific items you want. Or maybe you haven't made up your mind about whether to use fruit in the dessert, so you could wander to the market and discover that fresh blueberries were available, and it strikes you that a blueberry pie might be a good addition to the menu. The marketplace model similarly allows you to discover data sets that others have made available, which you weren't necessarily looking for, but can be valuable. As data proliferates in almost every business, the external value of that data will become much more visible in a marketplace model. Here's a good example.

Henning, a fantasy football buff from Norway, spent a lot of time constructing a list of *insiders* for each club from the English Football Premier League (soccer). These were all people from each club playing the fantasy football game. They included players and nonplaying staff. What Henning had figured out though was that if a player was injured, the first people who would react by dropping him from their fantasy football team would be the insiders from his club. In due course, Henning was able to disclose with high accuracy which players were injured long before clubs announced their squad for the weekend. And this was causing football clubs a lot of problems because their closely guarded team news for actual games was leaked, even though Henning was just doing it for the fantasy league. This is an excellent example of the externalities of data (and also, of course, of insider trading!). But these data externalities exist everywhere. Your business energy consumption may well be a surrogate for your financial performance, and very useful to potential investors. There may well be hundreds of data sets out there, which might be extremely useful for your business—but you don't know that they exist, what they might cost, or how to access them. What you need is a data marketplace with published and discoverable offerings.

From a users' point of view, we need to think about the way the data is accessed and analyzed. Do you need to query the data set for a specific point? Or do you need the whole data set? For example, you might want to check the weather on a Sunday morning before leaving home, if you just want to know what to wear. On the other hand, you might be designing smart weatherproof clothing, so you want the enter data set of the past five years of weather data. In the first instance, you can just query the data set for a single data point. In the second, you need access to the whole set. Also, is the data highly variable (e.g., stock position, weather in London), semipermanent (e.g., train time tables), or reasonably permanent (e.g., the data from the periodic table)?

We spoke about Scope 3 Emissions earlier—what are the other areas where you could see a data marketplace? Actually, we think there are any number of domains. The automotive industry is a particularly interesting area with manufacturers, service providers, second-hand sellers, insurers, and civic authorities all participants in the marketplace. What about city data marketplaces—where all urban data can be pooled and collected—already somewhat enabled through the London Data store. And it's this characteristic of data—to transcend industries and meaning that makes marketplaces especially useful. Other potential areas include health care

(NHS just launched a Data Register), natural resources, and research—especially in computational biology.

My colleagues at TCS research have actually created a data marketplace product (Dexam), which allows the setting up of a data exchange with discovery, description, pricing, and transactions. We just finished a proof of concept for this with a government agency in the UK, in a very interesting area around domestic pets and safety, to enable multiple entities within the government for sharing data. And I have no doubt that as ecosystems proliferate, the need for such marketplaces as foundational elements of ecosystems will surge.

PART 4

Optimize

CHAPTER 17

The Cruel World

The Four Horsemen of Change

What if you did nothing about digitizing your business? We all now know the many stories of great companies that went out of business because they *did nothing*, or they did too little. Nokia ignored the iPhone, Blockbuster ignored Netflix, and so on. But these are extreme examples of high-profile mistakes. Sometimes, the challenge is that we think we're digitizing our business, but we stop short of optimizing. This is equally risky. Plenty of taxi companies built apps, and every hotel had a website, but they were nonetheless caught flat-footed by ride sharing apps such as Lyft and Uber, or by room sharing solutions such as Airbnb. I was recently at a conference of health and social care firms, who were talking about digitization. But it was apparent that in their world, digitization meant putting their existing processes online and running everything exactly the same way but with less paper and more computers. This is a mistake, irrespective of what sector, industry, or function you're in. Digital technologies create new rules of competition, and not adapting fast enough always comes with the risk of extinction. Let's look at just four of the many ways that change will challenge us: exponential change, networked worlds, aging society, and climate change.

Exponential change: The word exponential has become much more familiar, thanks to the pandemic, and we know how this works now. But in a number of different ways, the speed of change is accelerating. There are two excellent books on this subject.

Exponential Organizations by Salim Ismail, and the more recent *Exponential* by Azeem Azhar who also writes the popular newsletter *Exponential View*. Salim Ismail recounted this story at the CogX 2019 event in London. Elon Musk wants to create Hyperloop as a rapid mass transport

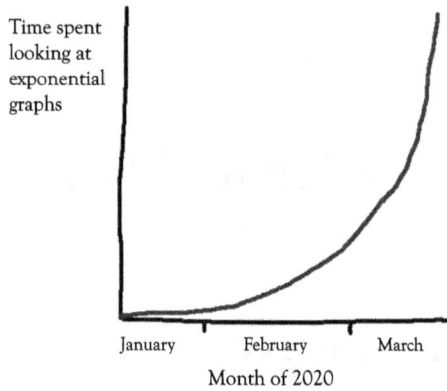

Figure 17.1 Exponential graphs

model, which basically involves putting people into a capsule and shooting them through a tube at high speed. When it was pointed out to Musk that accelerating and decelerating at that rate would kill a human being, he nodded and said "yes, it's a problem." *A* problem. Not even *the* problem. And Musk is continuing to invest deeply into many aspects of the Hyperloop. Musk is an excellent example of somebody who thinks exponentially. He sees the dramatically changed ground rules for an industry in the future, and works to get there, assuming that the exponentials will kick in, the world will catch up, and he's willing to be thought of as crazy and overoptimistic for a big chunk of that journey.

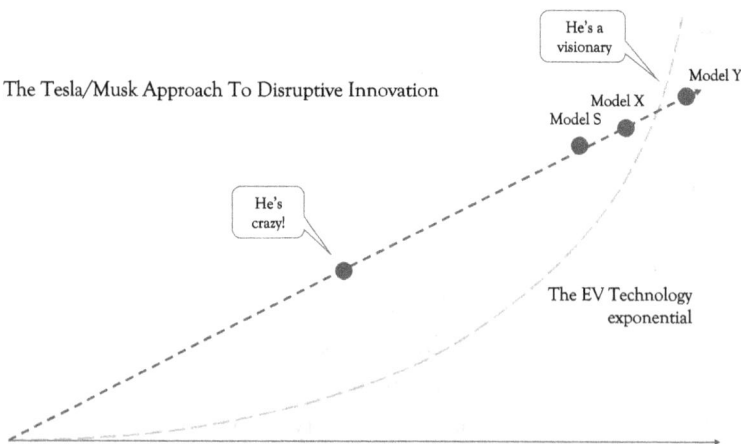

Figure 17.2 The Tesla approach to disruptive innovation

Similarly, in his recent book *Invent and Wander*, Jeff Bezos notes in his shareholders letter of 1997, that his book store model is not only successful, but is sitting on an incredible competitive advantage. His business, he says, depends on computing, bandwidth, and storage, and these are doubling in price performance ever 18, 12, and 9 months. There is therefore no way that any physical retailer can keep up with his business model, or scale, and he can turn this retailing engine to almost any category and be successful. He sees the exponential change and decides to ride it.

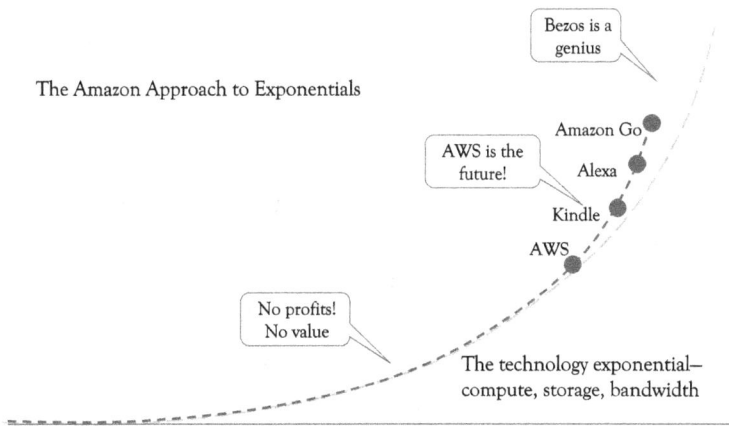

Figure 17.3 The Amazon approach to disruptive innovation

Networked world: Conceptually, a network is any set of nodes and relationships or connections between the nodes. A traditional social network involves people and personal or professional relationships. A digital social network implies that any two people on a digital platform are explicitly defined as connected or not, and this difference governs what you can do (send direct messages, see information, etc.). The train network is a set of nodes (stations) and relationships (train lines and connections). The World Wide Web is a supersized network of nodes (computers and servers) and relationships (data and information exchange), and your body is a network of nodes (cells and organs) and their relationships (information, oxygen, or blood flow). A football team is a network of players and their shared relationship which involves the rules of the game, their passing and moving, and common objective—to win a game.

Complex networks are like a network of networks. The global cargo network is a mesh of the road network, the train network, and the air and water networks. Ships can't travel by road or air, but an individual piece of cargo may traverse all the four networks in getting to its destination. Tiered networks are networks that have multiple layers of connections. For example, for the Internet to work, there needs to be a base connecting layer—so that computers can exchange data of any kind. Overlaying this is the set of Internet protocols that allow these computers to find each other and to send data in specific ways (involving disaggregated packets). And the Web is a third layer on top of the previous two, which involves using a specific set of markup languages that allow the data being shared to be presented and read in very specific ways and using a specific tool (a browser).

In the digital world, as more and more people, things, and processes are connected to each other, they are forming ever larger, more complex, and tiered networks. Networks have very specific properties that allow us to model and understand their behavior, but more importantly, the impact of changes across the network as well. The most commonly cited example of a network that's easy to visualize is a starling flock, as it weaves and bends and creates magical patterns in the sky. The flock has no leader, and no central brain or direction. Each bird can communicate with a very finite number of birds at any time. Yet, the network seems to have a life of its own, with both form and function. Not only is it beautiful, but the shapeshifting cloud formation keeps predators away. In our digital world, we can think of our ourselves as starlings in a giant network, and that everything we do in the digital world is the flap of a starlings' wings or a change of direction, that sends messages across the flock and in a tiny way, shapes the direction of the overall network.

Aging society: There are sociologists and economists who believe that the world might run out of people. There are others who believe that significant extensions of lifespans (in hundreds of years) is around the corner. These two premises are not as mutually exclusive as they might seem. The reality is that the world's population profile is changing. Up to 200 years ago, there was a steady, Malthusian growth rate of population, leading to a global population of a billion. Following the industrial revolution, population shot up to almost eight billion—an eightfold increase in a very short span of time. The reasons are many, including drop in infant and youth mortality, extension of life spans overall, and the industrial economic expansion, which creates both the demand and conditions for a larger population. This might be about to change. According to a number of estimates, we will reach peak population of around 9.7 billion just after the middle of the century, and from there, a potentially endless decline of population will kick in. The reasons again are to do with the 4th industrial revolution, a move to machines for production of goods and services, and a reduction in the demand for people. One of the direct implications of this will be the change in the demographic profile. We are going to live in aging societies. The 65+ age group will start to dominate the age distribution graph, and consequently, the dominant patterns of choice making, consumption, and lifestyles will morph. This change is already visible across Japan and Western Europe and will spread across the world. Alongside, we're going to see a revolution in health care, in part because the 65+ population account for the lion's share of all health care consumption.

Climate change: All of this presupposes that we have a planet, and if current trends continue unchecked, we may not. In 1987, Gro Harlem Brundtland, the Prime Minister of Norway, wrote *Our Common Future* arguing against the reckless consumption and focusing on sustainable development. For many years, this was a niche area and arguably one of those ideas that was on the very early stages of the exponential curve, so of course, everybody ignored it, despite Al Gore raising the profile of the issue. Today, it's probably the most dominant long-term agenda item for global leaders across the world. Sustainability can override almost every other consideration if it becomes a real global crisis. Here are two clear areas where we're already seeing a huge impact. The first is in climate goals and the control of emissions. Every company and organization across the world is signing up for net zero emissions over the next decades, and this is driving mega shifts in automobiles, from fuel to electric, in foods, from beef to plant-based substitutes, and many other areas of everyday life. The second is in the kind of regulation we're seeing—in Europe, for example, the Task Force for Climate-Related Disclosures (TCFD) requires every financial organization to disclose climate related risks for any long-term investments. This is no longer a matter for the head of sustainability, it's on the desk of the chief risk officer, which is a much more central role for banks. And if banks are having to report on this, it is very likely that they will want to see this data from the industries and companies that they are funding.

> Tip: Imagine a scenario of accelerated climate change, and think about how your business will adapt to a world which is 2 degrees higher in temperature. And explore how this plays out across every part of your business ecosystem.

This all may seem like a bit of a diversion, but these four aren't even the only factors that are driving the kind of sweeping changes we're seeing in the world today. Here is the reason that this wandering is core to the narrative of this book: collectively, these changes mean that things that have worked in the past won't work the same way going forward. Which sounds obvious, and trivial, but it also means that due to the multiple layers of change, much of expertise you've built so far is also becoming less useful in the future, at an accelerating pace. Which is a lot more significant—both organizationally, as well as individually. This is also what the author David Epstein calls *the cruel world hypotheses* in his book *Range*. The rewards for your accumulated experience are on a diminishing scale, in a cruel world. To visualize this, let's use an American stereotype. You may still be driving an SUV to a steakhouse, and then watching a football game on a big screen with three of your best friends, but your SUV is an electric one, which gets charged from the solar panels on your roof, your steak doesn't come from a cow at all but from plant extracts that are sourced from within 5 miles in vertical farms (but you can't tell the difference), and your three best friends are sitting in three different continents, watching the game with you in immersive 3D. Oh, and you're 110 years old, and you still have a full-time job, because you went back to university in your 80s and you're now a data exploration expert.

When all of this change happens very quickly even within the span of a single career, it creates additional problems. To understand, let's look at the calculus of change.

Evolution, Revolution, and the Calculus of Change

In 1999, Shawn Fanning, a 19-year-old software developer, created Napster—a peer-to-peer (P2P) file sharing format, specifically designed and optimized for sharing MP3 music files between users. You probably know that Napster changed the course of the music industry. At its peak, it enjoyed 80 million users. It significantly dented the profitability of the record labels. It co-opted its user community into what was essentially an extra-legal activity—ripping and sharing songs from audio CDs. College campuses banned Napster on their networks, and the rock band Metallica, among others, led the legal charge against the firm, which ultimately led to its demise. Nonetheless, the genie was out of the bottle. P2P networks of all other kinds flourished. From Rhapsody to Piratebay, they survive through to today. The economics of music publishing and distribution have never been the same again. This also paved the way for the emergence of legal streaming music—as Apple, Spotify, and others were able to step into a disrupted market with more elegant and legitimate solutions.

When music is converted from analog to digital, it's done by taking thousands of samples per second and converting them into discrete data items, which can be pieced together to recreate music. How many individual samples go into typical digital audio? Well *CD* quality has typically involved sampling at 44.1 KHz, or 44,100 samples per second. This is based on a mathematical relationship discovered by Harry Nyquist, at Bell Labs (among others). Today, we have tools for the lay user to tweak this ratio and sampling rate (you can define this rate while *ripping*[1] CDs on your desktop player, if this is legal in your country). Very high-quality audio can be sampled at 192 KHz. But this would not only create a very large file—hard to move around and infernally slow to stream, it would also be overkill for your human ears. Even the 44 KHz sampling was way too large for early digital formats, given the cost of memory, processing, and bandwidth, so we learned to compress this cleverly, in ways that we could dramatically reduce the size without making it feel different. This compression was done using *codecs*, short for compression–decompression. Using the same codec, you could decompress the files at the time of playing. One of the most well-known codecs is the family of codecs that are known by their creators, the Moving Picture Experts Group—or MPEG. This group created generations of codecs—MPEG1, MPEG2, and so on. Specifically, a codec called MPEG 1, Audio Layer III (namely, MP3) achieved fame and infamy in equal measure as a totem pole for disruption—as it was used by P2P networks for illegal distribution of audio files. (Note that MP4 is MPEG 4.)

Similar sampling is used for digitization of images and video as well. Higher rates of sampling ensure that the output is denser, but involves more data being captured, leading to higher file sizes. Lowering resolution ultimately leads to pixelation—where the sampling is small enough for our eyes to see the grain of the individual samples, or to notice the flaws in the audio.

Conceptually, therefore, the more fine-grained our sampling, the more realistic the sound. The better the output. When I'm asked whether the digital transformation is a revolution, or evolution or whether it even matters, I think about the story of media sampling, and measuring the rate of change. This relationship between the rate of sampling and the clarity of our experience is an important metaphor, when we talk about dealing with change.

The Industrial Revolution, Not the Industrial Evolution

The time from Thomas Newcomen's first steam engine in 1712 to Stephenson's rocket in 1829 via James Watt and others took almost 120 years. Which is approximately the time of the First Industrial Revolution. Benjamin Franklin's (and others') work on electricity ensured that the Second Industrial Revolution followed immediately, with the electrification of a lot of steam-powered machinery. During this entire time, new inventions spread at the rate of 5 miles per year because the primary mechanism was word of mouth. Only with the emergence of the telegraph did the spread of new technology accelerate. This phase of history from the early 1700s to the early 1900s witnessed progress at a blinding speed never seen before. It's only today that we can look back and classify it as slow, creeping, and almost glacial. Because, today, the world has changed as much or more in the past 30 years. Yet, we call it the industrial revolution, not the industrial evolution! Largely because it transformed the world as it existed—socially, economically, and geopolitically, in ways that the key players struggled to keep up with.

How Calculus Works

Calculus is a branch of math that deals with the measurement of changing variables. How do we figure out the speed of an accelerating object? Exactly when is the speed highest or lowest for a pendulum? Differential calculus works by measuring a variable speed over tiny bits of time, which are so small that the speed appears to be (or approximates to) constant over those tiny times, rather than variable.

This is analogous to our sampling challenge in our discussion on digital music earlier. If the period is small enough, then contiguous periods taken together give us a smooth transition from one note to the other. If the samples are too far apart, the sound appears broken and discontinuous.

The point is that dealing with change requires us to continuously measure and monitor that change and its impact on us. Doing so frequently, as in the example of audio sampling or following the principles of calculus, will allow us to be more aware of the changes as they occur. How frequent is good enough? Well that depends on the rate of change. The higher the change, the more frequent your measurement needs to be. In an extremely volatile situation such as a submarine in a war zone, you may need to keep your eye permanently on the radar screen, which is tracking the environment in real time.

Why is this relevant? Well, discontinuity is fundamentally hard to deal with. It's the step you didn't think was there, and often, it causes a stumble. Occasionally, a calamitous one. Therefore, a discontinuity that is caused by an actual invention or scientific breakthrough impacts the whole industry or world, but one caused by your inability to measure and monitor the rate of change is a threat just for your business.

In most aspects of everyday life, we do not encounter this kind of discontinuity, although there are plenty of occurrences in the world around us—you might find it if you were plotting the temperature versus volume of water between 95 and 105 degrees centigrade, for example. However, in terms of business changes and its measurement, these points of discontinuity are very hard to find. Any perceived discontinuity is actually likely to be a problem with our rate of sampling. If we don't measure this change often enough, it will feel like a step change. In the extreme case, if you went to sleep in 1987 and woke up 30 years later in 2017—you can imagine the absolute bewilderment you might face. It is very unlikely that a similar 30-year nap during the industrial revolution would have slapped you in the face in the same way.

Why Are We So Bad at Predictions?

We over-estimate the impact of technology in 2 years, and under-estimate the impact over 10
—Roy Amara, former President, The Institute for the Future.

There is a popular riddle about the king who offered a reward to a loyal subject—he offered him gold, land, titles, but the man just asked for grains of rice on a chess board. He just requested one grain on the first square, and double the amount on every successive square. According to the story, the king consented easily but was ruing his decision less than half way through the board. If you've heard this you probably know it's a very big number by the time we get to the 64th square of the board, but it may still surprise you that the number on the 64th square would be about 10 times the global production of rice today, or 461,168,602,000 metric tons!

We're wired to think linearly in time. Much like we see space—with a line of sight. We are taught compound interest, but we get it intellectually rather than viscerally. When you first encounter the classic rice grains and chessboard, you know that it'll be a big number. But you would be in a tiny minority if you could easily determine how big.

The way that the future unfolds is dramatically shaped by network effects. The progress of an idea depends on its cross-fertilization across people, geographies, disciplines, and collaborations. These collaborations are often the result of fortuitous clustering of ideas—such as the work of the nomadic mathematician Erdos who spent his life traveling from one associate's home to another discussing mathematics, or the story of the serial entrepreneur in Rhineland in the 1400s. Having failed with a business in mirrors, he was working in the wine industry, where the mechanical pressing of grapes had transformed the economics of winemaking. He took the wine press, and married it with a Chinese invention—movable type, to create the world's first printing press. His name was Johannes Gutenberg. Many historians ascribe the renaissance and the reformation to the invention of the printing press. This kind of leap is not easy to predict, not just for the kind of discontinuity they represent, but also because of these networked effects. We are trained to be specialists, becoming more and more narrow as we progress through our academic career, ending up more or less as stereotypes of our profession. Yet, human progress is driven by thousands of these collaborative, and often serendipitous, examples. And we live in a world today with ever-expanding connections, so it's not surprising that we have fallen behind significantly in our ability to understand how the network effects play out.

The opposite is also true. We are so caught up with trends that we don't factor in the kinks in the curve. Or to use Steve Jobs' phrase—the "ding in the universe." You can say that an iPhone-like device was sure to come along sooner or later. But given Nokia's dominance and 40 percent global market share, you would have bet your house on Nokia producing the next breakthrough device. Very few people saw the iPhone coming, but it created a discontinuous change that impacted almost every industry over the next decade.

Observing Discontinuity

Have there been any real points of discontinuity? Yes. Every scientific invention or significant discovery creates a tiny bit of discontinuity. But for them to create a discontinuity in the larger trajectory of business and society? There have arguably been two periods in the past 30 years where this has happened. The first was 1995, the year of adoption of Tim Berner's Lee's HTML as a standard. The second was 2007, the year of the launch of the smartphone. Here's a look at what else happened in these two periods:

1995: Yahoo founded, JavaScript released, the first Wiki launched, project Back-rub started (later to become Google), Netscape IPO, HTML standard adopted, Amazon.com goes live, Auction Web launches (later to become eBay), and the first all-digital (computerized) feature film movie Toy Story is released.

2007: iPhone launched, Hadoop (big data management) launched, GitHub started, Twitter launched, Android launched, Change.org launched, AT&T launched software-enabled networks, Amazon launched Kindle, Airbnb conceived in San Francisco, Palantir launched its first platform, work started on Watson at IBM, Intel introduced nonsilicon materials for microchips—thus giving Moore's law an extended lease of life. A year of discontinuity to match 1995!

While these two years stand out, the past three decades have undoubtedly seen an acceleration in the level of change across communication and production technologies. In times of accelerating change, your need to measure and monitor your environment and its impact on your business is ever more critical. The faster the change, the more frequent your measurement needs to be. You need a radar that is continuously scanning your environment—regulatory, competitive, technology, consumer, and others, for changes and points of apparent discontinuity. And your execution has to be designed for discontinuous times.

The Power of Small Change

The BBC's Digital Media Initiative was set up in 2008, to deliver digital archives, new databases and digital production tools. In May 2013, it was shelved, having burned through £125 million, and deemed a failure. Bear in mind that the BBC has an excellent and long-standing track record of delivering successful digital technology. Examples include the very successful iPlayer and the 100 percent coverage of every event during the 2012 Olympics. Clearly, this is not an organization unaccustomed to successfully delivering large complex projects against stiff deadlines.

A report from the Consultancy.uk website suggests that two-thirds of all-digital transformation projects fail. What sets digital projects, and specifically, digital transformation projects apart, and why do they fail so often? There are many well-cited reasons. They range from focusing only on the technology, to governance and stakeholder maturity, to a lack of connect with the customer and the frontline of the business. The more pertinent and forward-looking question may be, what does it take to make digital transformation and digital projects successful?

Over the past 25 years of working in the trenches on digital projects, and reviewing digital strategies at board levels, I've developed a strong olfactory sense of ideas that aren't going well and those where there's clearly a smell of success. In a nutshell, in my experience, it boils down to a simple credo—big vision, small action. This is a viewpoint you will see reflected in a lot of contemporary writing and thinking around lean and agile models (think big, start small, etc.), but somehow, while thinking big comes naturally, it's very hard for big companies to act small. Although I see signs that the smartest companies are recognizing the value of lean teams and working on small outcomes, which create momentum and the building blocks of great change, for most others, starting small is something that stays on the slides rather than finding its way into programs of work.

Don't get me wrong, big ideas are critical. They underscore the vision and direction in which we need to move. The big idea is the North Star of our journey. But you cannot negotiate even half a mile of unfriendly terrain with your eyes fixed on the North Star. And all too often, we fall into the trap of big idea and big action.

A typical idea of a big action is when a large company goes—"we are going to completely re-engineer the way we sell our widgets to our customers, across our 16 divisions and migrate from a direct to indirect sales network whilst improving our net promoter score and digitize our entire sales process while we're about it." You've all been there I'm sure. In the world of digital change and transformation, these big transformation initiatives are about as useful as a hippopotamus at a barbecue. Small execution has a number of advantages. Here are three of them.

Politics and Alignment

Big change requires the buy-in of many senior people, who may well have contradictory expectations and competing ambitions. Often the end product of a consensus is an unwieldy compromise, which no longer has the ability to deliver the benefits anticipated. By contrast, the small action looks at creating the smallest viable version of this change, may be in one division and one product line of a less prominent business unit. But with a little success and data, small change grows quickly. The power of digital is that it *is* possible to create successes and gather effective data on a small scale. According to its founder, the first version of WhatsApp was launched in three months with four developers working.

Speed

Speed is an immediate victim of the big change process. Likely timelines for getting alignment with senior teams can take months. It can even take months just to get the right people into the room, to discuss the key issues. A few years ago, I was working on a large complex digital program for a broadcaster with half a dozen workstreams, which had gone on for a year and a half with almost zero success. People were demotivated and change-resistant. One of the little things we tried was to take one of the workstreams and just focus on making that work over an eight-week timeframe. In two months, we had a success story, and suddenly, everybody wanted to be in on the journey. The entire program was completed in another six months.

Learning

In the large change programs, we spend a lot of time discussing the *right* answers with experts, and this is reflected in detailed plans, which assume that things will go as per schedule. This rarely happens, of course. Small change makes no such assumptions. Small action learns *on the job,* and consequently, it learns in real time. In the nascent and evolving digital landscape, often nobody's really an expert, so learning from expertise is immediately limited, anyway.

Remember, speed and size are relative. A few years ago, we were pitching a new and exciting technology-led change program to a client who are a big utility company. Our approach involved running programs of change, integrating complex backend systems, and creating an aggressive six-month program of work. One of the senior-most execs in the room from the client organization started the meeting by telling us how he along with a couple of his engineers had just spent the weekend *playing around* with a new location-based open-source utility that they found to be quite interesting and had built a pilot for replacing their existing clunky routing application and were planning to roll out the change to a small set of service teams within the next seven days. It suddenly made our six-month change program look very old world.

Think of a snowball that you start rolling down a snowy hillside, and how it gathers pace and bulk as it moves. This is how small change works. The opposite of this is the Sisyphean task of rolling a boulder up a hill. But better still, think of repairing a car by a committee of people with specialized and disparate skills taking the entire car apart, and then putting it back together again. This is how big change works. In the digital world, only one of these approaches is effective.

The next time you encounter a digital initiative, remember: politics, speed, and learning environments are some of the key reasons why it makes sense to commit small action, no matter how big the vision.

> Tip: For any project, practice thinking about the smallest possible viable implementation of the idea, and bring it to life to win support.

Optimization: Changing the Rules

If you've followed the arc of this book so far, we've spoken about the many ways we can connect, and based on the data the connections generate, quantify our businesses. It's only natural therefore that we should look at all this data and the picture it paints, and ask the question of how to improve our businesses.

Uber offers a simple example of this that all of us can relate to (most other similar services such as Ola and Lyft have similar models. I chose Uber as it has always been the brand that has defined the category). When you download and use the app, it offers you an instant benefit. You can book a taxi sitting in your living room or while still in the warmth of your restaurant, on a cold evening, in seconds. Similarly, drivers can find customers without having to be in their line of sight. This is the value of *connect*. But based on the millions of connections, Uber can map out the patterns of demand across a city and across time. And it can provide tips to drivers about where the demand is or isn't, at any given point. Uber might, for example, tell drivers in Washington DC to avoid Georgetown around lunchtimes, or London drivers might be told that Piccadilly Circus is quiet for customers on Friday mornings. They can obviously also accurately estimate the volume of demand and make decisions about driver recruitment as well. This is the value of quantification. But Uber doesn't stop there. For time and places where demand is significantly higher than supply, Uber creates surge pricing to tweak the economic model of its business. Surge pricing has many critiques, especially if you've been subject an astronomical price surge. But this is what economists call a market clearing price. When demand exceeds supply, you can raise prices till they do match. Uber can do this because it has gone through the connect and quantify stages very well, and also because it collects highly accurate geo-location data, so it can apply surge pricing to a very specific area, no more than a square kilometer, or even less. And for specific periods of time—which could be a few minutes. I've seen the surge pricing change in London when I walked a couple of hundred yards and tried after 5 minutes. The point is that you can tweak aspects of your business model in real time and in very specific and micro ways if you were a connected and quantified business.

Let me give you another favorite example. Sometime in early 2014, GM and Tesla both had problems with their cars, which could cause fires. GM, as per standard practice, announced a recall, which meant thousands of cars being brought in, fixed, and sent back out on the road again. Tesla, on the other hand, issued an over-the-air update, which upgraded the spark plug for almost 30,000 cars, and sent a message to the owners. They could do this because the cars were connected, and because there was software embedded into several components, allowing them to be changed via software updates. And the data generated by all these cars and the spark plugs themselves allowed Tesla to identify the problem and the potential solution. In this case, Tesla optimized the product life cycle model. This is an entirely new paradigm—something we may only have seen with computers and smartphones—products being updated over the air, and notably, products that might improve after you've bought them. For many products and customers, this is an offer worth paying for.

Today, we have a plethora of connections, and as we've seen earlier, mountains of data to access and exploit. But in order to effectively optimize our businesses, we need a few more tools in the toolkit. In the following sections, we'll look at agile working, the role of innovation, the importance of culture, and how to exploit AI and networks.

But first let's take a closer look at optimization and the connect–quantify–optimize (CQO) model.

CQO: Connect, Quantify, Optimize

We saw, in the example of taxi apps, how *connect* and *quantify* lead to the opportunity to *optimize*. We also saw how businesses such as Tesla use software to change how products behave. Note that the Tesla example is yet another way to connect. We're now connecting the product itself, and we know that when this works well, it leads to data and quantification. The average new car today has over 200 onboard computers and communicates continuously through satellite and other networks. A typical new vehicle will generate up to 25 gigabytes of data per hour. No wonder some people call the automobile a *data-center on wheels!*

What happens when you generate that much data from a product? You can quantify almost every aspect of the product's performance. How much distance the car has covered, how the brakes are working, how efficient the fuel consumption is, and the performance of hundreds of components and systems in the vehicle, and so on. Not just from each vehicle, but from the millions of vehicles on the road. You can therefore also quantify averages, deviations, and outliers, in terms of performance. You would know instantly if an individual vehicle was underperforming, or behaving differently from the rest, even before the owner of the car spotted any problems. You could also be alerted to the kind of manufacturing problems that we spoke about earlier with Tesla and GM, when you compare the performance data from vehicles on the road against the expected data sets. And suddenly, the decisions you make about your products and customers are driven by this data. You can alert an individual owner, or a set of owners, even if you can't upgrade the car over the air, as in the example earlier. This may change your customer engagement model—making you much more proactive rather than reactive. And given the continuously falling costs of technology, future versions of everyday products like shaving razors, and shoes could also be smart and connected.

It doesn't stop there. The power of data is also in its ability to tell the future, remember? So now you can also start estimating quite accurately exactly when an individual car, or a set of cars might be running into a problem. You could notify the owners, or update your distributors, train a set of mechanics, send out spare parts, or if possible, upgrade the product over the air, as Tesla did. Which means you've now also changed how you run your after sales business.

You can see therefore that our model of data-driven optimization can change your business model. In many cases where you're not dealing with customers, it may instead change your operating model, or the way you run a business function. Or simply allocate resources. For example, if you have an entry system in your office that is based on an employee access card, you should be able to find out how many people come to office, and when, on which days. Suppose now that rather than having to tap your card on a reader, your employees were comfortable using an app that simply recognized when you were in the office (putting aside the privacy concerns for just a minute). Or that the office doors worked with the proximity of the phone. The following things would then happen. First, your employees would get a better experience. One less card to carry and no more touching in and out of offices. Next you would get real-time information about your teams' dates and times across your offices. Over time, you might notice patterns in the data. For example, Wednesday is the busiest day in office, and there's a shortage of hot desks and meeting rooms, while Fridays are quiet, with only 25 percent capacity used. You could at this point create incentives for getting some people to come in on Friday instead of Wednesday, to smoothen out your infrastructure load. You could rethink your hot-desk approach based on these numbers. You could reduce your energy consumption on Fridays. TCS has launched a IOT-based product called Clever Energy to help companies achieve sustainability goals, by monitoring office energy usage, along these same lines.

You can apply the CQO model to almost any area. Consider the example of insurers who reward better driving via the use of apps. You download and use the app, thereby connecting your driving habits to the insurer via the app. The insurer gets the data and quantifies your driving behaviors and is able to rate and rank you against other drivers and also the likelihood that you might have an accident. Based on this, it can vary the price of your insurance, thereby rewarding you for safer driving habits, and so optimize their risk and commercial model. It's the same for health insurers such as Vitality, who track your fitness data, and reward you financially in terms of your health insurance premiums. The big shift here, if you've noticed is that rather than just get better at predicting the outcomes, insurers are starting to actually influence them. While the former can at best get you to parity with your competitors, the latter can be a sustainable differentiator for a far longer period.

Putting the Cart Before the Horse

I have always argued vociferously that it's business first and tech after. You must first sort out the business objective, change, process impact, and then select or customize the tool to the business needs. Of late, in the digital environment, I am learning to question and often invert this logic. Digital technologies are often far more end user friendly, adaptable, and personalized. Moreover, most users now have access to better technologies on their personal devices and the services they consume. The question therefore often becomes: "how do we use this cool technology at work as well?" In addition to this, new technology opens up opportunities that aren't obvious to businesses or end users. If an algorithm can spot the signs of domestic abuse from videos or photographs, for example, we may well be led by the technology, rather than wait for somebody to describe a specific use case for it, or if microbial analysis shows ways to defeat a persistent illness, we don't have to wait for a specific business case for application of the technology.

Tip: Make a habit of scanning emerging technologies to ask how it changes the realms of possibility for your business, service, or product.

CHAPTER 18

Disruption and the Business Model

The Original Digital Disruption

In the mid-1990s, Craig Newmark, a former programmer from IBM, created a mailing list that, inspired by the WELL (Whole Earth 'Lectronic Link, one of the earliest virtual communities), looked to allow software engineers in the Bay Area to share information about events. Within a year, by popular demand, job postings had been added, and an online version had been set up as Craigslist.org, in 1996. Over the next decade and beyond, Craigslist enjoyed meteoric growth, growing to new cities, adding categories, and drawing ever-larger audiences. It had a revenue model of charging $25 for job postings. Even today, Craigslist is the world's leading classifieds service in any medium. It posts some 80 million classified ads every month, with over one million job postings. It runs in 70 countries and with over 700 local sites.

When you think about the Craigslist model through the lens of disruption, here are some of the things that should become apparent. For the longest time, newspapers were the only way to reach large numbers of people if you wanted to rent an apartment, offer math tuition, or sell tickets for your neighborhood concert. And the reason that newspapers reached these audiences is because for most people, that *was* the primary way of finding out what was going on in their world. The content created the audiences, and the advertising monetized it. Classified ads were often the most lucrative part of the newspapers business on a revenue-per-column-inch basis. Craigslist not only blasted a hole through this model like a cannonball through a newspaper, but it did so with about 30 employees. The Internet allowed lean business models like Craigslist to build more direct connections between the network of buyers and sellers—without needing the mass audience engines that newspapers provided. It also allowed much faster and more efficient communication leading to a quicker consummation of the transaction. Craigslist essentially took away the most lucrative revenue stream of every newspaper. This is one of the most fundamental disruption patterns of the Internet. When suppliers and buyers are connected on a network, they will (or somebody will) find the most efficient way of bringing them together. This product might be answers to questions (Quora), all kinds of material products (Amazon and eBay), Videos (YouTube), or taxi rides (Uber). It is also a repeating pattern that this new model, typically less profitable than the old one, is eschewed by the incumbent, despite their greater market access, brand loyalty, and capital availability. We talk about *Uberization,* but really to give due to the original disruptor, we should be asking if your business might get *Craigslisted!*

> Tip: Look for any business model where an intermediary exists only to connect buyers and sellers, without adding much additional value. Or where the value used to exist, but has reduced. This is a recipe for disruption.

Putting the Auto Into Automobiles

What is common to Florida, California, Nevada, Michigan, Virginia, and Washington DC? In 2015, all of them allowed the testing of fully autonomous cars on their public roads. Some forms of robotic or autonomous cars are also now being tested in European countries. Let's take a moment to understand the enormity of this leap. Driving a car is a fiendishly difficult thing to do. It takes a typical adult over six months of regular practice to be really comfortable driving in cities. The number of distractions and challenges are immense. You have to watch for road signs, speed limits, traffic signals, the occasionally random behavior of other cars, the unpredictable behavior of pedestrians, children or pets running onto the road in a residential neighborhood, and all manner of potential hazards. And you do so while partially engaging your brain to also controlling your hands and legs to maneuver your car via the steering wheel, break, and accelerator, and in some cases, also via a clutch and a gearshift. It's a great testament to the brain that we can do this fluently and still have sufficient brain cycles left over to think, talk, or listen to music.

Given this complexity, it's quite mind boggling that we're close to being able to get autonomous cars on the road, which can negotiate all of this and do so better than the average human. On the other hand, perhaps we should recognize that while most of us, most of the time, can manage this, we're a long way away from being good enough collectively. There are 1.3 m deaths caused by road accidents and over 50 million accidents caused every year through human error. In other words, collectively, we're still quite rubbish at it. Speeding, alcohol, distraction, and drowsiness are among the biggest causes of human error. And human error is behind 94 percent of accidents in the United States.

Nonetheless, this is really putting almost everything we know to the test. A combination of sensors, networks, instructions, and reasoning. Perhaps one of the most sophisticated problems that artificial intelligence (AI) is currently attempting to solve.

Autonomous cars such as Google subsidiary WayMo's process between 500 MB and 1 GB of data per second. It is likely that a small fraction of that data will be retained and uploaded, but estimates of new data generated by autonomous cars are usually in petabytes. The LiDAR system (like RADAR with light instead of radio waves) helps location awareness to inches, not meters. It also needs to recognize things like arm signals of cyclists and hundreds of other subtle cues that can have huge consequences. The good news is that Google's cars have driven more than two million miles already. The average person in the United States drives 12,000 miles a year. Effectively, this is 160 years of an average human driving experience. And in the later chapter on AI, we'll discuss why this cumulative number is relevant—essentially because all cars learn from each other.

Service-Ization

In business-to-business models, the use of sensors has fundamentally changed the business model for many manufacturers, as products are shipping with hundreds of sensors. Armed with the data they are generating, manufacturers are now able to accurately identify, predict, and fix problems, significantly reducing the total cost of ownership of the product over its lifetime. And by retaining the ownership of the product, they are benefiting from this new model. This approach is now often referred to in now as service-ization, or servitization (I prefer the former). In this model, both the seller and buyer are invested in ensuring the best performance of the product over the period of its use. This is also called an *as a service* model. An industrial customer in this case would be buying the *engine as a service*—meaning they wouldn't be buying the asset, but effectively purchasing the use of the asset for a rental price. This also makes sense financially, as it reduces the complexity of investing capital and monitoring depreciation and allows buyers to simply make it an operating expense. The hardest part of this may be the organizational skill and culture change. One of the early movers, GE, were ultimately unsuccessful with the model underlining the difficulty for large businesses to convert industrial era successes to digital leadership.

Business models will nonetheless evolve by adding layers of services to existing and new products, and for many, the value of the service will outstrip the value of the product. You probably pay a dietician more for the service of tracking your weight and the feedback on your lifestyle and diet, than you do for the weighing scale itself. A smart weighing scale might just bundle the two together and give you the asset for free. Increasingly, companies will give you the asset for free in order to lock you into the service, a leasing model, which brings down your outlay but enables longer term revenue stream for the seller. The total cost of any product (say a sweater or a vacuum cleaner) will become clearer, and align value realization with costs—imagine a washing machine that you pay for with a combination of rental fees and pay per use. And you can extend this to hotel rooms, railway stations, rented cars, weather updates, flood control, air-conditioning, and more—all these are built on a core asset, and information-driven services layers, where maintenance and usage, cost, and value can all be tracked together.

> Tip: If you sell a product—try to articulate the entirety of services the product will deliver through its life, and how it would be if you could be paid for this lifetime of services, rather than a single payment up-front. How would this change your business?

The Anti-Scale Business

Technology impacts operating models in ways that we can't always antici-pate. There is a theory that the elevator enabled skyscrapers to be built and populated, which allowed companies to colocate thousands of employees in a single building, which made communication and administration effective enough for business at scale. So, the humble elevator enabled the great industrial giants of the 1960s and 1970s.

The next change was driven by computers, and it gave rise to another new operating model—colocation was no longer critical. This was even more scale-friendly, as any back-office labor-intensive processes could be done in remote locations—such as the Mid-West United States, India, Philippines, and others. Using this model, businesses quickly created shared services models, with enormous backend processing centralized into a single unit, and operating companies running the frontend and customer processes. Services industries especially were huge beneficiaries. Banks, airlines, hotels, and professional services firms, just to name a few.

This model also enabled a whole new breed of acquisitions, with the premise being efficiencies delivered by shared backend systems. Why have three customer call centers when one can suffice? Or three IT depart-ments or office services? History suggests that these have not always been effective, as any number of mergers have struggled to turn these projected cost savings into reality. The devil in the detail has often been the tradi-tional enterprise IT systems, which have often proved less flexible than anticipated. Getting data in and out and merging two large-scale CRM systems, for example, sounds much better on a white board than in prac-tice. I heard the CEO of Atom Bank (a new digital bank) speak about this problem in traditional banks. The reality is that unprecedented scale has not resulted in unprecedented efficiency. If you've tried calling a call center in recent times, you will know that few customers who have dealt with globally centralized customer care will have felt this efficiency!

One of the biggest obstacles to implementation of this kind of scale strategy is an inability to collaborate across departments and divisions. It's ironic that this problem is created by the efficiency-driven depart-mentalization of the current scaled enterprise model. In fact, individual departments often cover up for the perceived lack of support or capability in other departments, by replicating services and skills within their teams, effectively killing the original premise of shared services! We've all seen companies scaled to national levels, and then broadened out to adjacent industries. Banks for example wanted to offer a wide range of financial services and become a *one stop shop* for all your financial needs.

Today's cloud and API-enabled digital businesses tend to scale to a global rather than national level with just one product. The scale model is driven not by shared services and breadth but through automation and XaaS models. Businesses such as Transferwise, or ZipCar, do just one thing, but they do it at global scale. This is in some way simply the next stage of evolution of organizational design, brought about by digital tools. These digital business models are rendering the traditional model of scaling obsolete, by focusing on speed and time over costs.

Speed

Speed significantly trumps cost efficiency as a differentiator. I'm not suggesting efficiency is irrelevant, just that it's a constraint rather than variable to be optimized. In other words, beyond a certain level of efficiency, it ceases to be a point of differentiation. I met a traditional entertainment business in the UK who, as a part of their digital transformation, completely split the technology function by product. There was no *corporate* IT anymore. Their logic? The loss of efficiency was more than made up by the gains in speed to market. This is the operating model change many large businesses may need to make, to access the new scale models.

Valuing Consumers' Time

Cheaper isn't necessarily better. It also usually makes things less efficient for customers. Just think about calling your bank or utility company's customer care and having to explain your problem to each person as you get passed around from person to person. Thanks to the huge progress of personal technology with the Web and smartphones, consumers have started to value their own time much more. So essentially, telling customers that the process now costs another 5 pence less but takes 5 minutes more of their time is bad business. Most shareholder-driven large enterprises will still opt for the 5 pence less at the cost of the consumers' time. Successful digital businesses, on the other hand, are fundamentally on the same wavelength with consumers when it comes to time. Industrial era businesses tend to consciously choose cost efficiency over speed, while digital customers will gravitate toward time efficiency. The best digital businesses often provide both time and cost advantage, rather than offer tradeoff.

Tackling Disruption

Imagine that London's black cabs were run by a privately owned company, and that you are its CEO. You've been running a healthy, protected, and successful business for a long while. And suddenly, upstarts like Ola and Uber are challenging your business. You feel that they are bypassing regulations that you're obliged to follow. They have none of your fixed costs, or constraints, or asset base. They offer none of the service guarantees that you do. They are fundamentally less reliable. Their brand in age terms is barely out of its diapers, and often, like a recalcitrant adolescent, is often in the news for all the wrong reasons. And yet, your customers are flocking to their service and, not coincidentally, their lower prices. What would you do?

If you think this is a unique situation, take a look around, at recorded music, retail banking, payments, high-street retail, energy utilities, and television, to see examples of industries where this is playing out with minor variations. The question therefore is not if your industry will be *uberized* but when. The fact that *to uberize* has become an accepted term, and it has come to mean disruption rather than the act of calling a taxi says something about the primacy of this phenomenon. But across industries, similar seismic disruptions and value shifts are under way. How can you compete?

The example of city cabs vs ride-sharing apps is instructive because many of the arguments are visible and easy for us to understand. It's a story that has played out across a number of cities, between taxi companies, city legislators, and ride-hailing companies. Uber and Lyft aren't taxi companies, contrary to the clever one-liners you read about how the world largest cab company doesn't own cabs. In fact, that's why they don't own cabs, because they're not cab companies. This is not to suggest that they shouldn't give drivers employee benefits, or that they should not be subject to laws, just not the traditional taxi laws. Ride-hailing companies are the bits between the cabs, like the mortar between the bricks in a wall. This is true of many disruptors—they are not direct like-for-like competition. Much of the response to ride-hailing services by cab companies and local governments makes the mistake of treating them like a cab company. There's more: smartphones have been around since 2007, but London taxi drivers are still expected to pass *the Knowledge*, a course for memorizing London streets. Also, the electromechanical taximeter is often used by cities as a means of protecting the industry and controlling the supply, but a digital application with GPS can calculate fares, calculate routes, evaluate them, and also maintain an audit trail of routes covered.

We may sometimes get caught up in the status or dominance of our brands and products. The London Black cab, has perhaps suffered a stasis of evolution. Both from technology and design—in today's world, the five-passenger scenario is an outlier—there should be a smaller and lower-cost option with a lower environmental footprint.

> Tip: If you can see ways in which your service can be delivered at a lower cost, or with a better customer proposition, or with better technology, not doing so only invites others to try.

CHAPTER 19

Artificial Intelligence

The Next Era

What's common to stock trading, vacuum cleaning, language recognition, creating movie trailers, Mergers & Acquisitions (M&A) deal research, image recognition, data center energy consumption optimization, driving cars, and predicting hypoglycemic events in diabetes? Yes, you've probably guessed—they are all things that can and are being done with the help of artificial intelligence, or AI. AI has long been seen as the pinnacle of computing intelligence. It has taken many forms, some humanoid and some not. It spans popular culture, computer science, and fantasy fiction.

What Is AI?

The term AI was coined in the 1950s, largely based on the vision that computers could one day be as intelligent as humans. Today, as we get closer to this in some aspects, it seems to me that this definition is flawed. Partly because machine intelligence works fundamentally differently to human intelligence, and also because human intelligence is not a destination, just a milestone. There's no reason why a machine can't be smarter than humans, in principle.

Perhaps it's more constructive to think of AI as automating decision making. Rather than the finite and predetermined if-then-else options to choose from and the logic to be followed, in almost every other area of software, AI systems are designed to learn the decision logic, or the choices, or both. The evolution of chess playing computers highlights this perfectly.

In 1997, the IBM computer Deep Blue defeated Garry Kasparov in a best of six game match up. It was the first time a computer had won a match against a grandmaster. This was the result of 40 years of

evolution for chess-playing computers. The first generations of chess playing computers were built by chess-playing engineers who would embed
their knowledge and choices into a set of instructions. Consequently,
they were only as good as their programmers. Then, as computing power
grew, computers would essentially use brute force computing to calculate
all possible options over a multiple number of moves and effectively try
to out-compute humans. This worked against amateurs, but despite the
advancements in Moore's law, was quite limited against seasoned players
because good chess players play by pattern recognition and don't try to
compute all the moves anyway. But then came the breakthrough in the
1990s—when engineers figured out a way of making the program learn
from previous games, work out probabilities, as well as perform a high
number of calculations around the options. This was the version of Deep
Blue that finally defeated Kasparov. The chess story doesn't end there, but
we'll come back to it.

AI systems therefore combine a learning ability with inference-
making. For example: all cars have four wheels. The Ford Fiesta is a car.
Therefore, the Ford Fiesta has four wheels. It's intuitive for us to get to the
third statement given the first two. But giving a computer that capability
is harder. How did we get here? While AI is defined as a catch-all phrase,
the specific enabling technology that has brought us to AI as we know
it today is machine learning. As with the earlier chess example, allowing a machine to learn from the data available accelerates the capability
improvement of the system. So rather than try and design an intelligent
system, the focus is on designing a learning system, because computers
naturally process raw data much faster than humans.

There are two broad methods for machines to learn: supervised and
unsupervised. Supervised learning involves exposing an AI system to a
lot of labeled data (say pictures of cats), so that it can start to *recognize*
cats, and as importantly, distinguish between cats and *not cats*. This is
not different to how we teach children. A two-year-old growing up in
London (let's caller her Zianna) might mistake a cat for a dog. But we
keep showing her more examples, and quite soon, she understands how
to distinguish them.

But imagine a situation as in the story of *Jungle Book*, where a human
is growing up among the animals in the jungle (let's caller her Jane). She
has no supervision, but it is likely that soon enough, she will distinguish

between cats and dogs, and many other species that she is exposed to. She might not call them by any recognizable name. She might have a completely different way of telling them apart. Perhaps she smells them differently, knows their unique sounds, or can tell by their footprints. This is broadly how unsupervised learning works. The system is let loose on the data and allowed to make its own connections and inferences.

What's the difference? Supervised learning works better for some types of problems such as classification (cars vs. buses) and regression (rainfall projections). Unsupervised learning works for clustering (consumer segmentation) and association (customers who bought this, also bought that). Deep Blue was a form of supervised learning and it's defining feature was the ability to make chess decisions at a level of competence beyond that of any of its designers and engineers.

Chess-playing computers have evolved significantly since 1997. More modern versions, which have culminated in Alpha Zero from DeepMind (an Alphabet/Google company), have created a method where the computer is taught the rules of the game and then left alone to play millions of games against itself—44 million in the first nine hours, according to the company. As it does so, it starts to assign probability values for each move—in terms of its contribution to winning/losing games. It then starts to get better at a blindingly fast speed. Here's a statistic for you. In 2017, the world's leading chess-playing computer—Stockfish—could evaluate 70 million positions in a second. Alpha Zero took four hours to play *better chess* than Stockfish, from a standing start, and easily defeated Stockfish in a 100-game match.

Chess is a game where the same data is always available to all players (and observers). There is no data asymmetry, unlike card games, for example. Business has a lot of data asymmetry, so we need to add a few layers of understanding to this.

Key AI Concepts

What Is Reinforcement Learning?

This idea that the system learns at speed comes from reinforcement learning. The system is given a *reward* for the right answer and a *punishment* for the wrong one, which incentivizes the learning. A contribution to a winning position versus a resultant losing position for example. Note that this approach has at its foundation a notion of desired outcomes and a *good versus bad* framework. In our example of the children, Jane might learn faster than Zianna if her reward/punishment mechanism is a stronger one, for example, she gets scratched if she doesn't recognize a fox. (Note: I do not suggest any kind of harsh reward/punishment model for children!)

What Is an algorithm?

An algorithm is a sequence of steps and calculations that are required to get to a specific outcome. This is distinct from calculating a specific value, which is a formula. For example, how to reorganize a shelf of books in alphabetical order in the most efficient way may require an algorithm. Or separating socks by colors. Or estimating the area of a polygon. Even baking a cake with a recipe is an algorithm. A learning algorithm is one that looks at the success of previous decisions and uses it for future instances of the task.

What Is a Neural Network?

A group of algorithms working together is a neural network. Each performs specific tasks, collectively allowing the neural network to make decisions. Collectively, complex decisions can be made by relying on multiple layers of neural networks. GPT-3 is a neural network machine that is used for generating human-like text. GPT-3 uses hundreds of billions of probabilistic calculations to figure out what text will be most optimal.

What Is Deep Learning?

Deep learning is a subset of machine learning that uses multiple layers of neural networks. For instance, in order to recognize human faces in a photograph, you have to be able to first distinguish human faces from other oval shapes, such as balloons. Then you have to look at individual features, such as eyes, nose, shape and size of the face, and so on. Deep learning works by assigning these subproblems to the layers of neural networks so that collectively, the AI system cannot only identify whether or an object is a human face, but also recognize the same person across multiple photographs. You only have to go to Google Photos to see how this works, you can select a person, who has been identified and Google Photos can show you all the pictures among your thousands of snaps that have the person in them.

What AI Is Not

It's not a humanoid robot. There are many instances, especially in literature and films, where AI is embodied through a robot or a human. In the 2001 movie AI, for example, it's a little boy. While, the anthropomorphized versions may be more intuitive for us to understand. Think of the distinction between the body and the mind. It's hard for us to imagine the mind without associating it with a body or at least a brain. But in reality, the mind is an abstract concept and should ideally be form independent. Similarly, AI is a conceptual construct, and we should refrain from giving it any specific physical manifestation—human or otherwise.

AI and Optimization

In a way, AI is the logical culmination of the model that we've used in this book. In the cycle of connect–quantify–optimize, the AI kicks in with the optimization models. AI will help companies redefine themselves, morph their services and products, and reshape service bundles.

If you agree with the idea that the creative aspects of cognition are among the hardest for computers to emulate, and that strategy is essentially a creative exercise, then there may be need for humans and AI to work together in defining strategy for the foreseeable future. The best chess players in *Free Style Chess* are human–computer combination teams (centaurs, as they are called). But there is no doubt in my mind that the strategic winners will be those that can effectively harness AI at the core of the business, feed the engine via data generated and gathered at scale through all the digital interfaces of the company and other players, and continue to build more innovative interfaces with their customers. This is why, the end game for Google and Amazon is AI and if you consider the number of ways in which we already interact with these businesses and provide them with transactional and interactional data, you will no doubt immediately grasp their ability to build highly nourished AI engines.

Optimization is not formulaic, nor predictable. We don't know how we will optimize a business model—that is, tweak or transform it—until we get the interaction and continuous data stream. It's also a learning pattern where AI will very likely end up being much better than humans in the long term.

So, You Think the Brain Is Superior to the Computer?

Every discussion on the power of computers is bracketed by the comparison to the human brain and the dwarfing of any known computer by the fantastical power of the human brain. Estimates by Ray Kurzweil suggested a calculations-per-second (cps) capability of 10 quadrillion cps. And it runs on 20 watts of *power*. By comparison, the world's best computer today can do 34 quadrillion cps, but it occupies 720 sq. m of space, costs $390m to build and requires 24 megawatts of power. (I would recommend you that you read the great article referenced here, by Tim Urban.)[1]

The brain's sophistication is far, far ahead of the computers, considering all the miraculous things it can do. It is a giant neural network— capable of massively parallel processing—simultaneously collecting and processing huge amounts of disparate data. I'm tapping away on a laptop savoring the smell and taste of coffee while listening to music on a cold cloudy day in a warm cafe surrounded by art. The brain is simultaneously assimilating the olfactory, visual, aural, haptic, and environmental signals, without even trying too hard.

What does this tell us about the future of jobs? It would appear therefore that we are decades away from computers, which can replace brain functions and therefore, jobs. Let's look at this a little more closely though.

The exponential trajectory of computers and software will probably lead to affordable computers with the capacity of a human brain arriving by 2025, and more scarily, achieving the computing capacity of all humans put together by 2040. Note, this is looking at computing power alone, which is distinct from intelligence and from singularity. This is made possible by any number of individual developments and the collective effort of the computer science and software industry. Kevin Kelly[2] points to three key accelerators, apart from the well-known Moore's law. The evolution of graphics chips, which are capable of parallel processing—leading to the low-cost creation of neural networks; the growth of big data, which allows these ever more capable computers to be trained; and the development of deep learning—the layered and algorithmically driven learning process that brings much efficiency to how machines learn.

So, the hubris around the human brain may actually survive another few decades, and thereafter, the question might not be whether computers can be as good as humans but how much better than the human brain could the computer be. Initially estimated by Ray Kurzweil to be around 2045, but now believed by many futurists to be closer to 2060, the point of singularity is the point when computers actually surpass humans in intelligence, and set itself off on a path of exponential improvement. But that has been well argued and no doubt will be so again, including the moral, ethical, and societal challenges it will bring.

I actually want to look at the present and sound a note of warning to all those people still in the camp of *human brain hubris*. Let me start with another compliment to the brain. Consider this apocryphal discussion between two friends meeting after ages.

A: How have you been? What are you doing nowadays?
B: I'm great, I've been playing chess with myself for ages now.
A: Oh? How's that? Sounds a bit boring.
B: Oh no, it's great fun, I cheat all the time.
A: But don't you catch yourself?
B: Nah, I'm too clever.

One of the most amazing things about the brain is how it's wired to constructively fool us all the time. We only *think* we're seeing the things we are. In effect, the brain is continuously short-circuiting our complex processing and presenting simple answers. This is brilliantly covered by Kahneman[3] and many others. Because, if we had to process every single bit of information we encounter, we would never get through the day.

The brain allows us to focus by filtering out complexity through a series of tricks. Peripheral vision, selective memory, and many other sophisticated tricks are at play every minute to allow us to function normally. If you think about it, this is probably the brain's greatest trick—in building and maintaining this elaborate hoax that keeps up the fine balance between normalcy and what we would call insanity. Thereby allowing us to focus sharply on specific information that needs a much higher level of active processing.

And yet, put millions of all of these wonderful brains together, you discordant politics, bad electoral choices, wars, environmental catastrophe, stupidity at an industrial scale, and a human history so chockfull of poor decisions that you wonder how we ever got to here. You only have to speak with half a dozen employees of large companies to collect a legion of stories about and how the intelligence of organizations is often considerably less than the sum of the parts. There are plenty of tales about the smart individuals at Kodak who had actually created digital camera earlier than almost anywhere else. It would be fair to say that we haven't yet mastered the ability to put our brains together in any kind of reliably repeatable and synergistic way. Very much in trial-and-error mode.

This is one of the killer reasons why computers are soon going to better than humans. Computers have been designed to network, to share, pool, and exchange brain power. We moved from the original mainframe (one giant brain), to PCs (many small brains), to a truly cloud-based and networked era (many connected brains working collectively, much, much bigger than any one brain). One of the most obvious examples is blockchain. Another is in the example of the driverless car. Now, most of you might agree that, as of today, you would rather trust a human—(perhaps yourself) rather than a computer at the wheel of your car. And you may be right to do so. But here are two things to ponder. Your children will have to learn to drive all over again, from scratch. You might be able to give them some guidance, but realistically maybe 1 percent of your accumulated expertise behind the wheel will transfer to your kids, from your thousands of driving hours. Let's assume you hit an oil slick on the road and almost skid out of control. You may, from this experience, learn to recognize oil slicks, deal with them better, perhaps learn to avoid them or slow down. Unfortunately, only one brain will benefit from this—yours.

Every single person must learn this by experience. When a driverless car has a crash today because it mistakes a sky white truck against a bright sky, it also learns to make that distinction (or is made to). But importantly, this *upgrade* goes to every single car using the same system or brain. So, you are now the beneficiary of the accumulated learning of every car on the road that shares this common brain. Can you imagine the explosive rate of that learning?

Kevin Kelly talks about a number of different kinds of minds/brains that might ensue in the future, that are different from our own. If, like the airline industry, automotive companies agree to share this information—following every accident or near-miss, then you create a similar super-brain and start to get the benefit of every car on the road, irrespective of the manufacturer. Can you even compute how quickly your driverless car would start to learn? Nothing we currently know or can relate to prepare us for this exponential model of learning and improvement.

The human brain also betrays us in a number of ways. The quality of your training, upkeep, and performance management of the brain varies dramatically from person to person. Here are some ways where we're already behind computers, and I'm just going to consider one activity, driving:

Computation

The most obvious one, our computational abilities are already infinitesimally small, even compared to the average pocket calculator. This is obvious, but when you apply it to say, calculating the speed of braking to ensure you stop before you hit the car that's just popped out in front, but not so fast that you risk being hit by the car behind you, you're already no match for the computer. Jobs that computers have taken over on the basis of computation include programmatic advertisement buying and algorithmic trading.

Memory

Almost as apparent as the first point, nobody needs to be told that computers are better at remembering than we are. Although data stored in a drive does undergo degradation over time, in general, you would trust a computer to retain an overwhelmingly large amount of data. And as importantly, free from any cognitive biases. Human memory is, after all, incredibly selective! What computers lack is the ability to connect ideas in the way that human brains can. If you burnt your finger on a hot iron when you were five years, some part of your brain warns you while reaching for a completely different kind of heating appliance 50 years later. Even though you might have forgotten the original incident explicitly.

Sensing and Observation

Would you know if the grip on your tires has dropped by 10 percent? 5 percent? What if your engine is performing suboptimally, or if your brakes are 3 percent more loose than normal? Have you ever missed a speed limit sign as you come off a freeway or motorway? Have you ever realized with a fright that there was something in your blind spot? A computer, armed with sensors all around the car, is much less likely to miss an environmental hazard, vehicular data point, or road sign than you are. All this is before we factor in distractions, or less than perfect eyesight and hearing, and just unobservant driving. Other observation-based professions include security and flight navigation, where computers are already at work.

Reaction Time

Any driving instructor will tell you that the average reaction time is a tenth of a second for humans. In other words, at 40 mph, you will have covered 17 meters before your brain and body start to react. By the time you've actually slammed the brakes or managed to swerve the car—you may well be 20 to 25 meters down. By contrast, there is already evidence of autonomous vehicles being able to pre-empt a hazard and slow down. Even more so, if the crash involves another car using the same shared *brain*.

Judgment

The problem with our brains is that we rarely allow them to work to their potential. In the United States, in 2020, over 38,000 people were killed in traffic accidents. The top four causes of crashes in the United States are distracted driving, drunk driving, speeding, and reckless driving. The underlying causes may be stress, anger, tiredness, alcohol, or mobile phone distraction. The bottom line is that our emotional state dramatically impacts our judgment. And yet, we often use judgment as a way of bypassing complex data processing. Invaluable where the data doesn't exist, or the time available is too limited. But with the increasing quantification of the world, we may need less judgment and simply more processing, such as the *Hawk Eye* system in tennis.

Training

How long did it take you to learn to drive? A week? A month? Three? How long did it take you to be a good driver? Six months? This process will need to be repeated each time for each person. The collective cost is huge, and linear. Computers, as we've pointed out, can share learning via a giant virtual brain. Extending this analogy, in a number of jobs, automation will over time reduce training costs dramatically. This can include front desk operations, call centers, retail assistants, and many more. The time to train an AI has already gone from years to weeks.

> Tip: Think of any task, and then think of all the reasons why any two people might have different levels of capability for that same job. How many of these differences are human shortcomings that an AI system would not be encumbered by?

While we should agree that the human brain is awe inspiring for all it can do, it's also important to recognize its many limitations. Besides, the human brain has had an evolutionary head-start of some six million years. And the fact that we're having this discussion suggests that computers have reached some approximation of parity in about 60 odd years. Therefore, we shouldn't be under any illusion about how this will play out going forward. A last cautionary point—the various cognitive functions of the brain peak at different points of our lives—some as early as in our 20s and some later. But they do peak, and then we're on our way down!

So, AI represents a collective intelligence. It should not be benchmarked or bounded by human intelligence. It can already do a few things better than human brains, and definitely more consistently than humans. Fortunately, for most industries, there should be a significant phase of overlap during which computers are actually used to improve our own functioning. Our window of opportunity for the next decade is to become experts at exploiting this help.

At the same time, it is undoubtedly true that as of today, the best AI platforms perform well on incredibly narrow domains, which are either closed (such as games of chess and Go). And AI is far from perfect, so it's critical that we evaluate the cost of errors. Two key principles should apply here. The first is, what is the error expectation—that is, the probability of errors multiplied by the cost. The probability depends on the quality of the AI and the training data. Errors are likely to occur when the AI encounters data sets it has not been trained on. For autonomous vehicles, the cost of error is very high—in human lives. While the cost of error for an autonomous vacuum cleaner may be relatively low. The second principle is the comparison with human performance. The AI may not be perfect but does it improve on the current human performance benchmark? This is more ethically fraught than you would think. Imagine that in a world where all cars were autonomous, the United States registered 20,000 deaths per year through fatal accidents. This is significantly lower than the 38,000 deaths registered in 2020. However, if the accidents involving autonomous cars are of the kind that can easily be avoided by humans, such as mistaking a bus for an open road, or not recognizing a trailer as a moving vehicle, then they will always feel like unnecessary scenarios, which human drivers would easily have avoided. In essence, this is a form of a trolley problem—of choosing one set of mistakes over the other. Even if the macro numbers are better, every mishap will be a result of this choice. That's why, we need to tread carefully.

The Journey to AI

AI will find its way into every industry and almost every interface. Education, automotive, chess playing, voice assistants, customer services, these are just some examples. But what is the journey to AI? And what areas does it traverse? Let's look at the following picture.

The axes I've used in this example are (a) whether the computer is taught by humans or whether it learns on its own, which I've already explained earlier, and (b) whether it does things we can do or things it can't do. A quick note on the second axis. A lot of the reasons for using AI in business are to replace *expensive* or *error-prone* humans by cheaper and more consistent software. This includes areas of customer service and claims processing, for example. Or even early-stage driverless cars and making movie trailers. But the much larger and potentially unbounded opportunity lies in doing things that humans simply can't do, such as microsurgery and Mars exploration.

Almost all software historically have been about teaching computers to do what we can do. And this is where AI also starts. When we teach cars to drive, we do so with the underlying belief that we are only teaching them what we can do. I call this the zone of condescension. You can imagine why. It assumes that humans are better and computers can only do what we teach them to do.

However, once we start this journey, the technology evolves quite rapidly. For instance, there are already things that we have taught the car to do that we can't—for example, have a 360-degree vision. Or sense road conditions for ice. And communicate with other cars, for example. This is the zone of pride, in the way we might treat a child who we have taught, but who surpasses our own capabilities.

When we allow the software in the car to learn on its own, however, we enter a different zone. We may teach it to recognize traffic lights and deal with them accordingly. This is the zone of indulgence. The car has learned to do something that we can already do. We are happy for the car, but again, this is like watching our child learn to walk. Importantly though, the car is now learning on its own, so it can soon deal with a million different types of traffic lights.

But pretty soon, the AI goes into the zone where it's learning by itself to do things that we can't. For example—it may run transport networks at speeds that are impossible for humans to run safely. Or find ways to spot and fight cancer. I call this the zone of awe. Not just because of the kind of problems it can solve, because this zone is unbounded, but also because it could even decide which problems it chooses to solve. This is the gray area of singularity, of the fear of takeover by computers. But there is an ocean of useful purposes it can be put to. For the record, there isn't one single path—different types of AI can take different routes through this landscape.

Unsupervised learning

Zone of Indulgence Recognize cyclists	Zone of Awe High speed safe travel

Beyond human capability

Within human capability

Zone of Condescension Recognize Traffic Signals	Zone of Pride 360 Degree Vision

Supervised learning

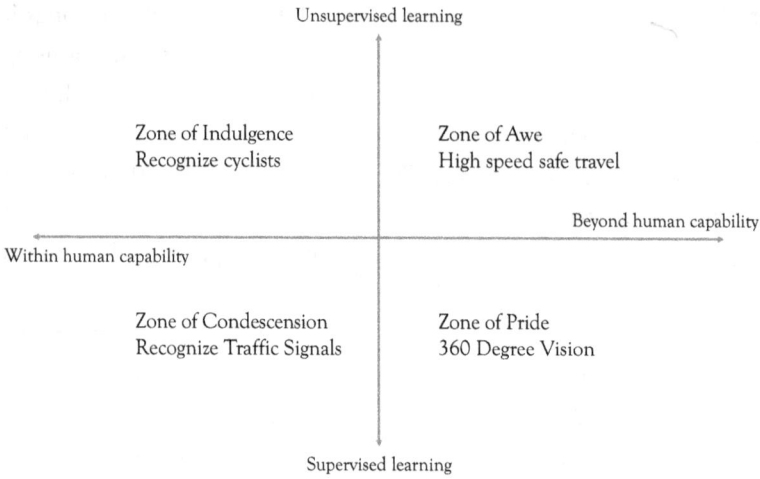

Figure 19.1 The journey to AI

Multisensory Environments

Perhaps the word is supersensory—that is, all the ways in which machines can sense beyond human capability. Here are some: human beings need light to see. Machines can use night vision, and heat sensing to *see* in the dark. A human can only process visual signals from one pair of eyes. A machine could have hundreds of eyes producing visual signals, which can be distributed geographically, across building, or a city, or even the world. A car can easily have 360-degree vision. By extension, machines can ingest any number of sensory inputs—sounds, temperature, sight, or smell, and it can do so remotely. A new satellite called Surface Water and Ocean Topography (SWOT) has recently been launched by NASA and the French space agency CNES. SWOT will be critical to monitoring the earth's fresh water. Monitoring all the earths fresh water is not a trivial task, but sensing via satellite helps!

The Role of Data

A brand-new AI system is like a human baby—with a great brain but zero ability. The baby evolves at an amazing pace by continuously absorbing signals from her environment delivered through her senses. The nascent AI brain needs to be similarly trained, exposed to a stream of data and contexts, and allowed to build up a base of competence and decision capability. The thing is, its ability to process and speed of learn is hundreds of times faster than the human brain, so it can, in a short while, do things in its narrow field, that an adult would struggle to do. Think of the chess computer playing millions of games against itself in a day. The availability of abundant data, and the evolution of tools to handle ever-larger quantities of data, is one more key enabler of the AI era. This is also why you will increasingly hear about synthetic data or the ability of AI systems to generate their own training data.

The Future of AI

We are still in the world of *narrow intelligence*—where AI engines are trained for specific tasks and are useless at others. For instance, a self-driving car's AI software may be amazing at negotiating rush hour traffic but would be useless if it were asked to perform customer service in a call center, or help with insurance claims processing. This is likely to continue for a while until we get to *general AI*, which more closely represents the human mind—where the intelligence can be pointed to any problem domain, with some effectiveness. The big question at that point is what happens after that. Because there is no reason for AI to stop evolving to levels far beyond human capabilities. Tim Urban's piece refers to this as super-intelligence—an IQ 100-fold superior to humans.

The Future of Jobs

Understandably, there is a lot of concern about the future of white-collar work in a world of AI. There are those who feel that this is the beginning of the end for work as we know it. There are two key strategies, I think, we as managers need to adopt to deal with this possible obsolescence.

The first is largely good news. Before AI starts to replace managers, there will be any number of roles where they enhance and augment us. Broadly speaking if a job is very routine and mechanical, the chances of being replaced by a software program, and not a particularly sophisticated one, are quite high. However, for doctors, drivers, and a host of other professions, in the short term, there could well be good news. The reason is very simple, humans are quite poor at a lot of tasks and AI will make us better. Take driving for example. Before AI displaces all drivers, we are likely to see a phase where AI works alongside drivers, and in selected environments, and we see a sharp decline in road accidents and fatalities. Similarly, AI should help doctors, and customer care professionals dramatically improve their output before they start replacing people. During this phase, we need to be able to be very good at using AI to improve our own performance.

The second phase will definitely be one of replacement. This will coincide with another boost in productivity—however, in this case, it may mean a boost by reducing the actual amount of human inputs for the same end goal. The problem with capitalism is that the benefits of this labor productivity don't go to the displaced workers. They go to the owners of the technology—that is, capital. This means that the only way in the current environment to benefit from the AI surge is to be on the right side of AI—in other words, you need to be owning, building, or investing in AI. There will be a range of new jobs that are created by AI, but usually, those jobs will require new skills and re-education, it won't be easy for a professional driver to participate in creating AI for self-driving cars. Nor will it be any easier for doctors, lawyers or marketing managers, unless you start early.

A note of caution: this is not as linear a journey as the earlier paragraph makes it seem. A recently released MIT report on the *Future of Work* calls out three ways in which technology impacts jobs. First, it enhances productivity, which releases people to do deliver more output by using better tools. Second, the overall improvement in productivity boosts income across the board, which leads to higher spends, and more goods and services being created and consumed. And third, by directly creating new jobs—in areas such as training AI algorithms. Each of these comes with their specific challenges, though. Productivity increase often translates into reduction of employees in large firms—thousands of automation programs are justified on the basis of the headcount reduction. Income increases, as we know from the same MIT report, are increasingly skewed in favor of the already wealthy, who have a lower marginal spend per additional dollar earned. And finally, the new jobs generated by emerging tech are often geographically removed from the old jobs, and require a different skill set. A factory worker in a Detroit production line does not have access to the software job in Germany or China that is now delivering the same component through a robotic process.

CHAPTER 20

Networks—We Live Inside Them

The Science of Networks

There is a cartoon about social networking—a funeral of a man with just five people in attendance, and somebody saying, " … but I don't understand, he had over 2000 Facebook friends!" It's funny when you see it through the eyes that believe a true friend, somebody who will come to your funeral, is worth more than hundreds of virtual, online, Facebook or effectively fake friends. I have an opposite view. I think it's pretty amazing that a person who has five friends at his funeral would have had 2,000 people who he knew and could connect with.

On another note, my friends are split between those who publish their birthdays on social media and those who expect their true friends to remember them. Since there's little chance of my remembering a thousand birthdays, I'm likely to depend on a diary or computer somewhere anyway, so it might as well be on Facebook as far as I'm concerned.

In both of these examples, we're talking about social networks and comparing strong and weak ties within networks in some ways. It is now broadly understood that both types of ties matter and bring different values. Strong ties offer *psychosocial support*—people you can turn to at times of stress or trouble. People who have the time for you. People who will remember your birthday and attend your funeral. In a professional sense, these could be your organizational allies, or the partner you've worked with for years, the head hunter who got you your last few jobs, or your former boss who mentors you. But there is another type of bond altogether—a loose tie, which also fills our social networks. The people who just know you well enough to wish you on Facebook, but won't attend your funeral. Or those who know you professionally but not well enough to follow your every move. Mark Granovetter's seminal work on *The Strength of Weak Ties*[1] changed our view of networks. He argued that in a number of areas, including marketing, politics, and other areas of persuasion such as getting a job, weak ties made a bigger contribution than strong ties. Strong ties usually form between like-minded people who share similar interests and often the same friends. By definition, therefore, the spread of new and radical ideas requires connections to people who aren't already converted—that is, people from a different group or a weak connect. Moreover, because these weak connections tend to be from different clusters, they create bridges between cliques in a network. Your chances of getting a job or getting widespread traction for a new idea are higher via the weak ties in your networks who may have access to new and different opportunities and people, rather than your strong ties who may move in roughly similar circles as you and may not have new opportunities and ideas beyond what you know yourself.

It may surprise you to note that Granovetter's work on Weak Ties predates Facebook or LinkedIn by over three decades. On the other hand, should it? Human social networks have existed from the days of cave dwellings of the hunter-gatherers hundreds of thousand years ago, and these dynamics have been largely true since then. Networks predate human beings as well. aspects of network theory, a more formalized branch of science in the past few decades, have been found to be true across the animal kingdom, evolutionary science, and even in microorganisms and individual cells. Albert-Laszlo Barabasi's work on network theory[2] started with the World Wide Web, but eventually encompassed biological networks in cells, physical networks in state transitions of substances as they moved from liquid to solid or vice versa, and many other human social networks, including the professional network of Hollywood films.

You may be familiar with the idea of the six degrees of separation—part parlor game, part myth—which looks to establish connections to the actor Kevin Bacon from any other actor, in less than six links. Although Kevin Bacon is irrevocably connected to this game, it was only a quirk of fate. Using now freely available data about movies and actors from IMDB, it's possible to actually analyze the Hollywood actors network. When Barabasi and his colleagues did the analysis, they found Kevin Bacon only ranks 876th in the six-degrees game—he had an average separation of 2.79 from any other actor. On the top spot, Rod Steiger had an average separation of 2.53, with Christopher Lee and Martin Sheen following in the podium places. This idea of the average distance is one metric that can be used to understand networks. Networks have a clustering coefficient, which shows the denseness of networks. A denser network may have higher clustering coefficient, and correspondingly, a lower average distance between any two nodes. Networks also have size, which is the number of nodes in the network. Taken together you could start to understand the behavior of a network. Information would travel faster through a densely connected network and the speed at which it reaches the end would depend on the density and size. Think of gossip in a well-networked small town, where news of an affair might travel overnight. Whereas if you take the entire political system as a network that is much bigger and much less densely interconnected—news of a scandal may travel at varying speeds and take much longer to reach everybody.

Scale-free networks are networks where the distribution of connections between nodes is not just uneven, they are strongly skewed. Rather than a random distribution (which you might represent as a bell curve), they are asymptotic curves with a few nodes at a very high number and many in a long tail. Imagine the income distribution of all people in any capitalistic society arranged by levels of income. You'll have a very long tail of people with low to medium incomes and a very high spike at one end where a very small number of people enjoy incredible wealth. A much-cited recent report by Oxfam reported that the eight richest people in the world have the same cumulative wealth as the bottom 50 percent of the population. If you plotted the world's income distribution, therefore, you would see a scale free network, which displays this kind of *power law* distribution. There is a mathematical expression of the power law, and these kinds of power laws are exhibited all around us—in biological cells, social networks such as Facebook, and professional networks such as Hollywood. They are ubiquitous, and we need to understand them better.

Living in the Network

Aether was the old word for the stuff that fills the sky, and over time, it came to mean air, as in vanished into the ether. Information that could travel at high speeds through the air was always a sought-after fantasy of scientists, so Robert Metcalfe was probably jumping the gun when he named his new invention Ethernet on May 22, 1973. What he meant by ether was actually coaxial cables, which would carry packets of information in a network. Nonetheless, Metcalfe's Ethernet would go on to become the dominant model for networking between computers for the next few decades. If you've used a corporate LAN or WAN, you've probably used an Ethernet network. Over the 1980s and 1990s, corporate networks across the world adopted Ethernet networks at scale, and as we speak, this remains close to a $20 billion annual market.

Much of the Internet sits on top of Ethernet networks—by using TCP/IP protocol as a layer over Ethernet, which is the physical layer. The Internet connections don't actually care what the physical layer is. They work over wireless, and wired connections and dramatically expand the reach of networks beyond LAN and WAN, to a universal and publicly accessible network. The Internet needs little introduction, but it isn't the only network we use today, by far. We typically use Wi-Fi networks in our houses—which connect to the Internet but also increasingly connect our TVs, entertainment systems, music systems, computers, phones, and other devices such as Amazon Echo and Ring Doorbells. The cars we drive today include networks, which connect the many onboard computers to each other and to the outside world. Effectively, we move from network to network as we go from home to car to work. City centers and public places are also increasingly connected to the Internet via Wi-Fi networks, or we are forced to use more expensive mobile (3G and 4G) networks. One way or another, we are permanently connected in these layered networks. Which means information can flow through these networks in ever more efficient and creative ways.

The human body is a network too, our brains are seen as one of the most sophisticated neural networks, and something we are only recently able to model. As medicine embraces nanotechnology and we start to connect the body through implants and measuring tools, we will make ourselves into a more explicit network as well, and become another extension of the network of networks that our lives are increasingly starting to represent. As you can see, while for much of human history our social networks has been abstract concepts, the last 50 years have seen a physical manifestation of our social networks that has grown in unimaginable ways. And riding on the physical network is the increasingly sophisticated information, social, and professional networks, which make our worlds work.

Understanding the Value of Networks: Looking at the World Differently

Understanding how networks work therefore may be key to our being able to best use and exploit the networked world we find ourselves living in. Thanks to the hyper-connected nature of the world, we can now look at a lot of our major infrastructure and industrial systems as networks. For example, instead of the mechanical view of the asset intensive environments and moving parts in transport, we could look at our transport system as a network with nodes, links, and behaviors. This would allow us to better model how information flows through these networks. In any case, the interplay of all the elements of this network make it far too complex to model using traditional structural means.

We are seeing some of the network effects playing out today. One of the ideas Robert Metcalfe is also credited with is the eponymous Metcalfe's law, which states that the value of a (telecommunication) network is proportional to the square of the number of connected users of the system. Putting aside the exact mathematical equation, which has been questioned and modified, this is intuitively easy to understand. The first person to have a telephone has a useless device as she can't call anybody. The value jumps as a second and third person get phones. The more nodes on a network the more valuable it becomes. Today's autonomous cars struggle because they also have to account for the random and unpredictable behavior of human-driven vehicles on the road. The value of autonomous vehicles goes up the more autonomous vehicles there are on the road—they become safer, they exchange information, and learn collectively and they update each other based on information received from their environment.

In their excellent 2001 HBR article *Where Value Lives in a Networked World*, Mohanbir Sawhney and Deval Parikh identified the idea of network intelligence as something to be harnessed by decision makers in complex environments. They argue that the value of the network is that the intelligence and tasks do not have to be colocated on a network. Intelligence can be pooled and centralized or decentralized as required. The way client server systems work or browsers work today is very indicative of this. You have the distributed, fragmented frontend intelligence that deals with users in each click, touch, and transaction. And you have the aggregated and centralized intelligence at the back end. In Sawhney's words, the middle bits are the dumb conduits.

Malcom Gladwell talks about nodes or people who become hubs in a network[3]—they have the maximum number of connections, and he also talks about mavens, who attract information and knowledge. Connectors and mavens can only exist in networks, by definition. You might see plenty of this in the startup network in Silicon Valley or even inside your business. Usually, some people become very good at being connectors—they have been around longer and know everybody in the business. They have a lot of social capital and can be very powerful to any project or initiative in spreading ideas. You also have the mavens who everybody goes to, to discuss new ideas or information.

One of the great things about networks is their resilience. In a network, thanks to the presence of multiple and therefore individually redundant connections, the loss of a node usually does not significantly slow down the performance of the network. A server or a computer going down on the Internet would barely be noticed by a systems administrator today, because everything is usually backed up and distributed with built-in redundancy. The Internet's underlying network architecture was in part a response to a need for a highly resilient system that could not be brought down by simply bombing a *network brain*, in a war. This kind of network intelligence that functions without a brain is plentiful in nature. You see it in the working of many species, including ant and bee colonies. You can see it work at breathtaking speed and motion in the murmurations of a starling cloud. Or you can see it in the glacially slow formations of *slime mold*, which are single cell organisms. The starling murmurations work in a way that each starling's movements only impact the seven starlings closest to itself, but this is transmitted quickly. Because of this, any reaction to external stimulus such as a bird of prey can spread very quickly through a flock of starlings, and the whole cloud can react very quickly, but almost as an intelligent unit *independent* of the size of the flock. Slime mold naturally forms a line toward food, but despite no brain or advanced communication capability, it can collectively find the most efficient way out of a maze or replicate railway systems. These are both intelligent and resilient because removing one part of the slime or any starling from the flock will not change the behavior or sophistication of the network.

Thanks to the hyper-connectivity we're seeing across the world, and the flow of abundant data, it would not be wrong to say businesses increasingly represent complex networks. Rather than terms such as supply chain, we should probably think supply network. In fact, my colleague Frank Diana, a futurist, has researched this at length and he looks at the emergence of ecosystems, rather than industries, in the way that business is increasingly organized. Ecosystems are essentially networks and they follow the laws of networks. This gives us entirely new ways in which to think of optimizing businesses. By opening up APIs, and enabling coupled functionality, technology firms are always looking to become ecosystem hubs and extract network value.

Tip: For any digital project, map out every stakeholder involved in ensuring the output you seek, and how they are interconnected. What binds these entities together and how can you move to the center of the network?

Networks in the Real World

We will see more and more application of network theory and insights across industries and problem domains, as ecosystems proliferate. Whether we are looking at payments networks or health care systems, network properties such as resilience, network intelligence, and the use of network metrics and behaviors will be used to model these industries and solutions rather than the traditional ones we've seen historically. Here are four interesting areas to consider.

Blockchain

Blockchain isn't new anymore. It is technology that is clearly born of the network. In order to make transactions truly robust, blockchain uses the network to get over the two key challenges of fraud—either the computer that is recording a transaction is compromised and under the control of a malicious third party or the miscreant tries to go back and change previous records to show a different version of transactions.

In essence, Blockchain is a distributed ledger where transactions or records are stacked in blocks and then stored in every computer on the network. Moreover, the security is also distributed across the network as each block is encrypted more than once, and finally, it is put through a cryptographic process to which the answer can only be found by trial and error. All the networks in the network try to solve it, and when one does, the solution is verified by others in the network. This element of chance means there is no single computer *in charge*. Finally, the *hash* or encrypted value of each such solution is made the identifying string of the next block—so the chain ensures that you can't tamper with previous blocks without changing all subsequent values. At present, blockchain is ideally suited for high-value transactions, where speed is not essential. Land Registry, tracking valuable jewels, and post-trade settlement are good examples. In future, I've no doubt that our identities will be stored in a blockchain-like network solution.

Future Organization Structures

The traditional organization structure has been under fire, as it can often appear to be out of step with the needs of organizations today. By creating a hierarchy, it forces a decision system that is not necessarily in line with its environment. For example, capital allocation is done by a senior financial expert who may not understand how emerging technology is changing the return on capital across range of initiatives. Investment in new disruptive products and solutions may often be derailed by owners of existing products, or senior people whose career is locked into the success of the current products and processes. A number of options have been mooted—most organizations have strived to grow flatter and some have even tried holacracies as a structural principle. The self-organizing principle of holacracy will undoubtedly have many critics and its share of failures. But ultimately, modeling the organization as a resilient network is a very powerful idea. This would allow the network intelligence to play a key role in the behavior of the firm, along with any individual decision makers.

Shifting Value in Broadcasting and Media

For the broadcast media industry, the network value model translates value moving to the two ends of the content network. Companies either need to own the content, or they need to own the consumer. Content owners are those who are making more investments into original content— HBO and the BBC have always been investors in new content, but today, every single company, from Netflix, to Amazon Prime, is following suit. At the other end, those who own the consumer are the ones who have a relationship with the individual consumer. These are the platforms with registered users, or providers with a billing relationship with customers. Set top box providers or OTT platforms all belong here. The value is leaving the middle bit—the world of traditional TV channels, for example—who have historically made money by connecting content providers to platforms. In the UK, Sky's business model has, in a very large part, been driven by its monopolistic stranglehold on premier league football content. The pure content distribution and packaging model of channels (and magazines) is gone. If you're going to be in the media business—you either need to own original content or the viewer relationship, or both.

Is there no value in distribution then? Well, tools like Paper.li and Del. icio.us allow the aggregation itself to be democratized. This is basically software-eating media-eating software! Also, players like Business Insider, Outbrain and Bleacher Report, or Quartz are trying hard to build a business that truly exploits the new distribution in different ways. Quartz has been described as an API, as fundamental to their business model is the assumption that people don't directly visit their website.

Darwin's Paradox is the phenomenon by which despite occupying under a thousandth of the words surface, the coral reefs support 25 percent of all marine species. A part of the answer lies in the cooperation and symbiotic relationships between species in the reefs. Some algae families that absorb carbon dioxide provide the corals with growth materials in exchange for CO_2 and host services, protection, and access to sunlight. This cooperation is now recognized as being just as critical to the evolutionary system as competition.[4] So, it is that all the tools and products that use Google's map API actually make the maps stronger, and often better, by adding data back to it. Or the Twitter ecosystem, which works in a similar way, relies on third parties for many of its sustaining innovations.

Open-Source Software

Since the time of Linus Torvalds, and later Netscape, in the 1990s, the open-source movement has championed the cause of software that can be freely used and distributed. Not just to use, but to modify, and build on. This has led to some of the most commonly used software across the world, especially the Apache Foundation, which has over 227 million lines of code and over $22bn worth of software available to the world at large. This is only possible through the power of the network—in connecting and enabling collaboration across these thousands of software experts across the world and creating shared value across hundreds of problem areas of software development, deployment, and maintenance.

The Dark Side

Sadly, terrorism too, uses similar network effects—by creating media storms through acts of barbarism, they look to heighten fear and anxiety. Other network participants such as politicians sometimes use divisive policies, which sustains localized discrimination leading to alienation and strengthening the extremists. The media and politicians are unwitting cooperators in this network. Today's terrorist networks are rarely command and control organizations. Instead, like platform organizations, they allow individuals and groups around the world to share a common platform for furthering their individual agendas.

CHAPTER 21

Making Agile Work for the Rest of Us

If you're like me, you've been in turn impressed by the clarity of agile thinking, bemused by the jargon, amused by the rituals, and occasionally frightened by the fanaticism of some of its missionaries, this may be a useful chapter for you.

There is no doubt that if used correctly and in the right context, the agile methodology can deliver great results. But it's equally important that we understand how to use it correctly and the conditions under which agile thrives. It's also important to appreciate some of the challenges you will face, working with Agile and its practitioners. This chapter is written for you if you are not a developer, an agile expert, a scrum master, or even agile familiar.

A Quick Recap

For the uninitiated, traditional *waterfall* software development involves a linear flow through requirements, design, development, testing, and deployment. This makes the quality of the final software highly dependent on the quality of the requirements captured. It also makes requirements mistakes expensive to fix as they are discovered as late as the testing stage. This worked well within enterprises when you could define the software and make people follow the system, but less so when you're dealing with consumers (and increasingly even employees) who have the choice of using alternative tools. Moreover, the pace of change means that often the requirements fixed or known at the start, even by the end users. And the waterfall model is highly change-unfriendly. Even small changes often bring a significant increase in cost and time required. Consequently, the software development process suffers from delays, cost escalations, and a mountain of documentation.

According to the *Agile Manifesto*,[1] agile is a way of developing software in a manner that delivers on time, on value, and embraces the reality of change in requirements. It also strips away the scaffolding of documentation, and relies much more heavily on working software. It focuses on the maturity of the team—to plan, execute, and reflect, and values simplicity and face-to-face communication. It is a complete counterpoint to the waterfall model.

In order to execute against these principles, the agile approach uses a number of techniques and measures. These include sprints, scrums, burn down charts, velocity, stories and epics, retrospectives, minimum viable products, and many others. Often, when we first engage with agile teams, this is what we see—the visible rituals of agile, which can make us feel like we've stumbled into a meeting of a secret cult.

A New Religion

It may not be a cult, but it is my view that for enterprises, adopting agile is deceptively difficult. In fact, adopting the rituals is easy. Adopting the philosophy is incredibly trickier. It requires a huge mind shift. It's harder than supporting a new football team or changing your favorite sport. It requires you to think about things in a new way, almost from ground up. It's important that we understand this and be conscious of both the benefits, which are many, and the significant challenges, which I'll try to highlight shortly.

Why It's Better

First, though, let's remind ourselves of the benefits of agile. The reality is that in the fast-changing world we live and work in, today, linear and waterfall projects invariably run the risk of going through an endless series of change requests, rebudgeting, and re-design effort. Especially when it comes to new services and products, market innovations and digital initiatives where breakthrough technologies and new user behaviors are commonplace. Even traditional enterprise software—such as sales and CRM systems are better delivered with an agile approach for these reasons.

So, Why Is Agile So Hard?

No Agile Team Is an Island

The first challenge to consider is how to make the enterprise agile. If the development team is switching to agile, the enterprise needs to as well. As such, it's not just a software development methodology, it becomes an enterprise manifesto as well. It becomes the way you launch new software, roll out new processes, and make changes to the business. If you think that you can run an agile IT team without impacting the way the rest of the business runs, you will be running the ship aground very quickly. You may need to create a very clear handshake (or API!) between the agile and non-agile parts of the business anyway, especially during the transition, but getting the business to think agile is critical.

The Challenge of Metrics

The CFO has a problem. In a traditional waterfall world, she knew how much money she was investing and what the expected returns were. Most agile experts will tell you that you can't pinpoint exactly what features will be delivered 12 or 18 months down the line because the methodology is an emergent one. The reality is that given the likelihood of changes that any project would go through, the agile project will invariably deliver more than the waterfall one. But the CFO, nonetheless, has to make this leap of faith. The industry needs some metrics, which have gathered data across a number of projects and established via benchmarks, which might say, for example, that agile projects on average deliver 20 percent more than waterfall projects. This does not seem to exist today. In fact, many agile projects can't even tell the CFO what budget they will burn through over 12 to 18 months.

Similarly, the business owner would like to ensure that the product gets to market before that of the competitor, or that the CRM upgrade is delivered at an industry standard cost. What she will probably get from her agile team is a response about the team finding its own velocity and burn rate. These are interfaces that need to be built, or the CFO and business owner have to be agile exponents themselves, and work out their own metrics for investment, risk, and competitive parameters.

This is not to say that agile projects don't have metrics. There are plenty of metrics used by agile teams across the board. In my experience, these are very useful for the self-regulation and management of the agile team, but less useful for external reporting. Often, therefore, the misguided marketing manager is asking for a Gantt chart for the app so that he can share it with the external agencies, much to the bemusement of the scrum master.

Realistically, any business needs metrics for development and product creation that are predictable, comparable (with other businesses), and compatible (with other metrics that exist in the business). Agile projects often struggle to deliver all of these metrics outside of the core development metrics, which are internal to the team. Unless, of course, the organization itself switches to an agile mindset and uses different metrics.

Practical Stuff—Contracts

As a significant percentage of IT work is delivered via external partners— software shops, agencies or system integrators (SIs), these relationships are governed by contracts. Most of these contracts are still written with traditional, pre-agile work structures, and accordingly, their governance structures and risk-reward mechanisms are not aligned with agile philosophies. Potentially, we could get to more iterative contracting to reflect the agile approach and philosophy. A big part of this is the issue of trust. Agile works on mutual trust and maturity, and most contracts are still built on more adversarial terms.

Skill and Maturity Levels

Last but certainly not the least, you need to think hard about the skill levels and maturity. If you're used to a more traditional waterfall approach, using a global software partner, the chances are you have *software factories* set up. The factory model works at scale, as the name suggests, with each individual focused on a very specific area of a *production line* of software. The agile world is more like a lab where each individual's contribution is key and the level of individual, both from skill and maturity perspectives is much higher. You are expecting this person to manage without documentation, and productive driven by personal motivation. It is very dangerous to take an erstwhile waterfall model and switch it to an agile one keeping the same team and skills in place. There is no reason why this should work. I have seen projects suffer because of the important differences between project managers and scrum masters. A large project with multiple teams and external stakeholders may need both. Needless to say, leadership styles will differ significantly across the two models.

This does not imply that agile can't be done at scale, or with teams distributed across the world. Organizations that have made the investment and upskilled teams and processes are increasingly delivering software faster than ever before.

Forewarned Is Forearmed

In most of the projects that I have seen at close quarters, the teams have had to hit a number of challenges in the early stages of projects and had to conduct a specific meeting with all stakeholders where the primary question was "what did *you* mean by agile?" If you're in a situation where you're being told to run an agile program, I hope this chapter has pointed you in the direction of what to look out for and guard against so that you can benefit from the power of agile while addressing all the challenges.

Of all these challenges, the one that is probably the most difficult and yet the most subtle is the need to look past the rituals of agile and embrace the philosophy. Without this, you will always be out of tune in an agile orchestra.

> Tip: In any agile project with a new set of people, invest time in a sprint zero model, to discuss what agile processes and rituals the team will follow and why, and what the shared goals are for the project.

The Myth of Fail Fast

Anybody who has come within hearing distance of a digital project will have heard the phrase *fail fast*. It can sound as though if you haven't failed fast or aspired to, you really shouldn't call yourself a digital professional! Here's what you should consider whenever you think about fail fast.

Fail fast assumes that you start quickly, and small, such as gathering a core of people who can follow the two-pizza rule and rolling up your sleeves and getting to work. If it requires a three-month negotiation to get resources released from various cross-departmental teams, requesting for space and funding, and having to satisfy more stakeholders than the number of people in the project, you're not fast already.

In order to fail fast, we need to be able to define failure, have a plan of action for when it happens, and ensure that data gathering is baked in. In actuality, most projects live in the twilight, where some things have worked, and others haven't. Failing, therefore, is rarely absolute, and our definition needs much more fine-tuning. There are hundreds of little failures on the way to success. Only occasionally will you see a real and obvious pivoting moment, or a significant failure. For the rest, it's all about deciphering and solving little failures. AB testing is your best friend there, not the glory of fail fast.

Only companies that truly believe in innovation and experimentation reward failures. For the rest, people get moved out, budgets get taken away, and nobody wants to talk about it anymore. Does your organization have a reward for the best failure? I prefer the term learn fast, and succeed fast, which requires focus on the metrics, data, and instrumentation, which would allow us to build the learning model.

Remember that the mantra of "fail fast, scale quickly" implies an easy transition into the next stage. What you might experience in reality might be fail a little, succeed a little, fail a little, succeed a little, for a long time till you're ready to scale. Are you ready to handle it if your second, third, and fourth attempts are also fast failures? I once met a CEO of a startup who had an audacious plan involving launching satellites. He said that over two years, he pitched it to over a 100 investors, and they all said no. But he persisted till somebody did say yes. Most corporations don't have the patience for two failures, let alone a 102. James Dyson went through 5,127 prototypes before his first market-ready model of vacuum cleaner.[2]

Should you be actually to the point of scaling, you're going to have to take some hard calls. This may involve diverting resources from other projects, and shutting down other initiatives to focus on the one initiative to scale. Money may not be the problem, but management bandwidth and attention usually are. Also, ensuring that everybody gets behind an idea is a critical construct. This is where in the typical corporate environment, politics or organizational priorities get in the way.

The lean method is absolutely the way you build a new product and service. And today's tools, technologies, connectivity, and access make it easy to go through those cycles in days rather than in months. The point is, a startup expects to fail. Entrepreneurs are terminally optimistic risk takers who fly in the face of logic. Therefore, startups are ready to fail over and over again because that is the way to success. A large corporate is built on some past success and no longer wants or expects to fail. It's just like we grew up and forgot what it was like to make mistakes and learn as children.

> Tip: Make sure you have a product owner and a scrum master, but not a project manager for your agile team.

CHAPTER 22

The Transformation Agenda

Although this book is not written as a guide to transformation, it is undoubtedly a form of root-and-branch optimization. Here are some thoughts to keep in mind if you find yourself in a digital transformation program.

From TOM to EOM

The target operating model (TOM) is the staple of transformation environments. The logic being, you have an initial operating model and you enter a transitional phase, driven by internal and external change, and you emerge with a new *target* operating model. It's an excellent construct and very useful for delivering change.

In today's digital environment, though, the idea of the TOM is challenged because of a number of reasons.

It assumes that the change is a finite and one-time activity. This is no longer true. You enter a phase of virtualization of your servers and networks, and before you finish that, you're in the middle of the mobility revolution, by the time you combine cloud and mobility to create another transformation and everybody is talking about big data and social analytics. And then there's the Internet of things (IOT), machine to machine and machine learning, and AI waiting to happen. And areas such as automation and cyber-resilience are always going to be ongoing initiatives. Which points do you pick as the start and end of the change?

If the change is not a finite or a single event, what do you assume as your end state or *target* environment? And if you can't define a target environment, then how can you create a TOM? Would it not be outdated even as you were implementing it?

After all, each of these technologies, from mobile, to cloud, to IOT, and AI—often lead to deep changes in business and operating models.

Yet, many organizations see it essentially as platform upgrades or technology changes.

The reality is that your digital transformation project is not a one-time exercise, there is no end state, and your TOM may be in need of an update by the time it's bedded in. The likely scenario is that there will be multiple waves of transformation. And here onward, they will all be digital.

Perhaps the right way to think about this is as an evolving operating model (EOM), rather than a TOM. What would the key features of an EOM be? Here are two key ones, though there are many more, such as business agility, instrumentation, and others.

> Tip: Consider building a model where an annual cost of change is built into the operating cost of the business, rather than treat it as a capital expenditure.

Building a Change Capability

At the core of this is the creation of a culture of change adaptability. I've consulted for many organizations where the smallest change has to be handled with kid gloves and is a source of anxiety and stress. And yet, these are all big changes we're talking about, so there's a lot of work to be done to make people change-friendly, and to make the change, people-friendly. From the way employee contracts are written, to the role of human resources (HR) in driving awareness, education, self-empowerment, and counseling. Leadership needs to invest in the right skills and enough time to grow into this change culture.

Based on my experience, there are parts of the world, such as the UK and Europe, where this would be a harder process than, say, in Asia. European business cultures are much more rigid about roles and function, and these are often defended by regulation. Also, in Europe, there is often a much higher premium on matching exact experience to a role, rather than bet on adaptability. One of the ways to address this is to balance the majority of such fixed role people with a handful of adaptors—people who can foster a pro-change environment within the business.

Funding Change

Can you build in the cost of change into your cost of running the business? Rather than the one hit capital expense of a digital transformation project, budget for change annually, that lines of business (LOBs) and divisions can draw from, with the right checks and balances to ensure governance is provided. There is every likelihood that each of the next five years will demand significant changes to some part of your business or the other. Rather than running it as a giant centralized project, or forcing this on to individual departments and LOBs who may not value this investment, organizations should explore creating a funding bucket, which is made available to teams based on their justification, against a stated vision. But this investment is locked down for change efforts and cannot be used for other purposes.

According to Statista, $1.5tn will be spent on digital transformation efforts worldwide, in 2021. Back in 2014, the BBC announced a program of saving £48m and reinvesting at least £29m of that into digital transformation services across channels, mobile and digital journalism. At the same period, there were banks in the UK spending upward of £500m on IT alone, to enable its digital transformation. Big bang approaches are still popular. But, the time may have come for alternative approaches.

Strong Cultures Kill Market Signals

At a small roundtable event I moderated around disruption in payments, one of the participants, a senior banker from a major high street, suggested that some of the hype around Fintech disruption was overblown. He pointed to the size of the high street bank he represented and the mountain faced by the challenger(s). At which point, one of the other participants pointed out rather succinctly that the argument was identical to Nokia's in 2008.

We now know that smart engineers in Kodak had already built prototypes of digital cameras as early as 1975, and were ignored. Nokia knew about Apple's iPhone plans from studying their patent filings, but dismissed it as they didn't think Apple could seriously create a competitive mobile phone. Despite having delivered a winning design with the

Mustang, Ford's leadership refused to take Hal Sperlich seriously with his idea of a vehicle that was something "between a car and a truck," even though his idea was backed by research. He was, in fact, fired. He moved to the struggling Chrysler along with Iacocca and delivered a very successful minivan.[1] The Xerox PARC team had created GUI, and personal computers, in the early 1970s. In 2000, Blockbuster rejected the overtures from Netflix when it was looking for a partnership. The list goes on.

At the core of this is business culture. Most very successful companies tend to build strong cultures. There is a high intensity of alignment with the *story* or the narrative arc of the company. This is conveyed in the corporate storytelling and converted to legend in the corridors. The leaders connect strongly to this narrative and use it as a motivational and performance tool. Often, this enables companies to retain employees even when they aren't the best paymasters—because the employees are emotionally bought in to the narrative. I have seen and worked in more than one such organization. You can almost smell the culture of the company in the discussions and everyday interactions. The dark side to these strong-culture companies is that they become the antibodies against any kind of change agent. Even as they protect the corporate culture from dilution as the business grows, they become the enemies of any disruption signals. You may have seen this in your businesses. Disagreeing with the corporate narrative is seen as career limiting. You may be treated as harmless and misguided, but worse, you may be viewed with suspicion and seen as a troublemaker.

Usually, people who join strong-culture companies realize very quickly whether they fit or not. Often you see a lot of early attrition as people quickly recognize the lack of cultural fit. How do these companies capture disruptive signals then? Very difficult, unless the CEO or somebody at the very top has an epiphany. One such instance, now well recorded for posterity, is the e-mail Bill Gates sent to his staff in 1995, recognizing the need for a complete turnaround with respect to the Internet and Netscape.[2] But in most companies, it's the crazy middle manager who, like the example of Sperlich, takes their ideas elsewhere. For strong-culture companies, often the only way is for the leadership to recognize the disruption signal. Some tend to set up an entity outside the purview and influence of the existing corporate structure, and more importantly, culture. GE set up a separate technology development team in Silicon Valley but still wasn't able to escape the gravitational pull of its old culture.

To state the blindingly obvious, therefore, the lack of dissenting voices should be one of the biggest signs of doomed incumbency. Beware the strong culture corporation, therefore, you may just be the proverbial frog in the gently heating water of change, slowly getting boiled by the very culture that made you strong.

To enable market signals to percolate through, view your business from the perspective of your customer/client. Ask yourself what problem you are solving. Then ask—what are the other ways is the customer solving this problem? How will this problem change in future? Who else is looking to partially or tangentially solve the problem? You needn't stop at the customer. Ideally, you could be studying the environment, regulations, competition, technology trends, to try and understand how your business might be changing. And when you identify something that suggests a shift, you may need to ask yourself the bigger question—what business are we in?

> Tip: Take a day to think like the competition. How would you attack and outmaneuver your own company if you were working for the competition? If you can think of ways this is possible, it's likely that so can a few competitors.

Blurry Boundaries: Rethinking Homes

Where do technology majors, utility companies, media businesses, retailers, and consumer electronics and appliances all compete for the same market? That's right—in your living room, for control over your home network. Yet, with multiple industries now set up to deliver smart services into a connected home, the onus of managing across all these services falls on the consumer, and there is little capability or support for this.

The biggest challenge is often the connectivity inside the home. Apart from well-documented standards problems—the Digital Living Network Alliance (DLNA) tried and failed—there are also a plethora of home networking options, none of them perfect. Wired options such as Cat5 are expensive unless done at the time of building or refurbishment. Wireless options—Wi-Fi and Zigbee being the most popular suffer from reliability issues—which can be an irritation for media or disastrous for health care. This problem may ultimately be resolved with a combination of cloud and 5G technologies.

With each industry choosing to go its own way, you, the consumer, are left with a scenario that involves multiple, disparate digital services each with its own security framework. When you then consider a household with four or more people, the number of passwords and access control challenges quickly escalate to unmanageable proportions. Further, imagine the confusion if you need to leave your home for seven days for a family holiday, when you want the lights to go on for two hours every day, but you need your medical support team to know that they won't get any readings from your in-home sensors. Clearly, the connected home environment does not pass the user centricity, or the simplicity test.

What about technology support for the connected home? For example, when you can't get your smartphone to work with your connected thermostat, who do you call? The thermostat provider? The mobile phone maker? Your home Wi-Fi router provider? A handyman?

In recent years, here has been a huge spike in the number and sophistication of connected services and products being launched in the market. Consider smart energy: smart thermostats are a crowded market with varying sophistication and pricing. From Google Nest, to Netatmo, Tado, or Honeywell (Evohome). In the UK, every major utility provider— British Gas, EDF, and others, can give you a smart thermostat solution. Depending on how much you want to spend you can have multiple zones in your home and control the heating for each, separately, from your phone, and control hot water separately.

There are also plenty of interesting and connected home automation products. I had the opportunity to meet Ring the connected door bell company, but also, smart cameras, smart locks, (even more) smart fridges, and to top it all, a house that tweets. Connected blood sugar monitors, smart mirrors, and other medical devices are now easily available. You can see how quickly we can go from the wonderful to the whimsical and back to serious.

When new market spaces such as connected homes open up, it redefines the business model for incumbents. For utility businesses that are stuck between uncontrollable input costs and regulatory price caps, this offers a new business model. Apple, Google, and Amazon are all focused on a slice of the home network, which tells you how lucrative this could be. But above all, the connect home represents a blurring of boundaries of a number of disparate businesses, creation of entirely new services, and entirely new data-driven relationships with end customers. These are classic patterns of the digital era.

Talent and the Myth of Millennials

My daughter, Maya, was taken to a jewelers' store at the age of five, in Lucknow, India, as her grandparents wanted to buy her a pair of earrings. After patiently sitting with her mother looking at options for a few minutes, at this very traditional establishment, where handcrafted designs are meticulously displayed under glass counters under the watchful eye of the proprietors of the store, she said—"I don't like any of these, Mama, can't we just order them on Amazon?" No wonder that they say that any technology you encounter before the age of four is not considered technology, it's just the way the world is.

As I've just done, usually at some point in any discussion about digital business, one of the participants will talk about his or her young/teenaged/ university going children to make a point about new behaviors, the new order, or to highlight the gap between the generations, digitally speaking. Young people no longer use e-mail, or even Facebook—it's all snapchat and beyond. They don't have TVs, and they don't believe in paying for content. Little kids have all tried to swipe TV screens or thought that a magazine was a broken iPad. By now, everybody has a story like this at home.

After all, this digital generational divide is the *sine qua non* of the transformation that businesses are facing. Most stereotypes exist for a reason, and it is therefore true that in order to understand the world of tomorrow, we must understand the new mindset and habits of the children and youth of today. Sadly, in too many discussions, this becomes the conclusion. A perfunctory discussion in a board room where everybody around the table agrees that kids today are all different, and hence, the only way to understand the new directions for the business, we need to hire a few of *them*.

Millennials Are Not the Answer

Millennials are said to be *practical credentialists* who accumulate experiences and skills with a very directed goal of creating a *packaged self.* They also identify common patterns in the way this generation deals with intimacy and identity and are given to the narcissistic effect for example of looking at your own image in a videoconference on Skype, for example. All of this is useful while marketing services and products to this generation.

Equally, as a prospective employer, there are things you have to do to attract, and perhaps more importantly, retain the new generation of colleagues into your business—from bring your own device (BYOD) policies to transparent cultures, or entrepreneurial opportunities. But to treat the hiring of millennials as the answer to your digital transformation—be it process, culture, or strategy, is, at best lazy and at worst, value destructive.

Over half the workforce are already millennials. Whether or not this reflects your company, remember that the millennial generation includes everybody born from the early 1980s onward. In other words, the earliest millennials are 40 years old today. Many of them have been working for over a decade and a half. To further highlight this, almost 70 percent of the population of India is under 40. That's about 800 million people. In fact, the average population of the UK is around 40, which is now a millennial age. There's no point talking about millennials as the workforce of tomorrow. They are, in fact, the workforce of today. Which means that they are a part of the problem. Even the next generation—aka Gen Z, are now an established part of the workforce.

Second, many 30-year-olds are very set in their ways. Yes, they may be mobile-friendly and have more digital lifestyles than their older colleagues (more Netflix and less satellite television), but in their own way, they have become set in their ways and can't adjust to the next wave of change. By and large, once people enter the workforce, and fall into a routine, many start to become institutionalized and find it hard to change the way they do things. Teachers, nurses, store managers, and sales executives all face this challenge of cultural sclerosis. I've worked with more than one organization where the average age is relatively low, including that of the leadership team. But even in these organizations, the change propensity is low, almost as though the dominant culture is of a generation that has only seen one way of doing things and has never needed to change.

Third, the digital generation is not homogenous. If we simply consider the pace of change and technology evolution, then it would follow that with the acceleration in technology, generations will get narrower, that is, every 4 to 5 years would need to be considered a new generation. Just consider the how the *Web* generation who grew up in the 1990s compares with the mobile generation—who grew up after the iPhone, and you can see they are vastly different.

The mobile generation, or as Tammy Erickson calls it in her HBR article, the re-generation,[3] was born around 1995 or later, is the generation that wants to swipe every screen they come across, and expects to be on multiple screens at the same time. This generation is all about expectations of connectivity and being willing participants in solving issues— digital activists or at least aware of their role and influence by the virtue of a simple *like*. If we are to go with this classification, this generation has just entered the workforce armed with the ability to touch-text like their parents could touch-type. This generation can start a flash mob or start a revolution from their handheld devices as the Arab spring showed.

I Am a 50 Something Teenager

Every morning when I wake up, I reach for the phone almost as my eyes start to focus. I check the news, WhatsApp messages, LinkedIn, Facebook, and football gossip. I make no apologies for this, although my wife often calls me a *teenager* because I look at my phone too often (in my defense, I don't reply in grunts or lock myself in my room for long periods). I am, however, pro-change. I'm wary of routine, and I enjoy diversity. My music, my books, and my bank are all digital. I enjoy staying connected, and experimenting with new apps, platforms, or situations. And I know there are hundreds, even thousands, of people like me who are capable of staying ahead of the curve when it comes to technology, or new businesses. These are all people who exhibit the behaviors stereotypically associated with millennials or Gen Z.

A close friend who runs a business with over 10,000 employees once told me about how he and his leadership team take decisions on WhatsApp—by running a single group where everybody can participate. Ashok Vaswani, the CEO of Barclays Retail Bank in the UK, has said he learned to code and hack. The ability to adopt and use new technology isn't purely a function of age.

If you're looking to hire the people who will take your organization into the next era, stay clear of the oversimplification of *hiring young people*, and instead ignore the age and focus on change capability, and ability to deal with the unknown. You may well find more young people fitting that description, but using age as a surrogate of change capability is a risky recruiting strategy.

According to research by the executive search firm Korn Ferry, *born digital leaders,* that is, millennials, are narrow in their skillset and fast rising in digital native companies. *Going digital* leaders, who are also sometimes called digital immigrants, are typically broad based and bring more rounded leadership traits, including critical skills such as influencing, navigation, and relationships. As the report says,

> But it's the rare executive from the independent, non-hierarchical, pure-play digital world who succeeds in a traditional corporate setting. Fit becomes critical to determine if such leaders will succeed in a traditional company's culture—as well as the region or country of employ.

Tip: While hiring, look for demonstrated ability to change, rather than age, when exploring digital talent.

PART 5

Connect, Quantify, Optimize

CHAPTER 23

Connect Quantify Optimize—The Model

The CQO Model

We saw in Part 2 how digital interfaces are reshaping our businesses. Be it mobile, Web, or sensors, we are increasingly opening up more and more interfaces with our customers, employees, and the environment. All of these connections then create gargantuan amounts of data that allow us to quantify our business in entirely new ways, which we covered in Part 3. And based on all of this data, we should be able to intelligently optimize our businesses as we discussed in Part 4. In this section, let's look at the application of the connect, quantify, and optimize (CQO) model.

The start point for almost every good digital project has been the rethinking of a customer journey. Let's say the check in process for an airline, or the mortgage application for a bank. Let's consider the very hypothetical scenario of a near-perfect digital project where everything is done as it should be. In this world, the team studies the user (customer) behavior thoroughly, through observation and conversation, builds personas around the types of users, and understands their current user journey, and both stated and latent needs, and challenges with the current journey. They then run design sprints to recreate this customer journey. This effort typically culminates a new mobile app or a website redesign. It could end up improving an existing product or creating a new one. For example, a bank could redefine its mortgage processes across the board, or it could create a new 24-hour montage product for specific types of customers. In either case, it is likely that some existing processes will be modified, and some new processes will need to be created. The customer application form and the way it is submitted could be modified. But a new straight through process could be created, which brings the assessors, surveyors, and lawyers together in a much more efficient manner.

If all of this goes well, you now have a customer using and valuing a new digital interface. But additionally, the data output means that every step of your customer journey becomes visible. You might, for example, notice that most of your customers for your new product are using more expensive devices and are looking at high-end properties. Which in turn might lead you to focusing your sales and marketing efforts. But what if it led to your creating a two-tiered product structure for meeting the needs of a broader segment?

This is where it gets interesting because the data may throw up many more insights, which could reshape your business in big and small ways. In a 24-hour mortgage product, you might, for instance, realize notice from your data set that you have a set of customers who apply for a mortgage only after selecting a property. This may allow you to provide ancillary services to this set of people beyond the mortgage—such as bringing together an ecosystem of trusted providers aimed at helping customers to repair and redecorate, or even provide ancillary loans for specific house-related activities. This stage may actually end up changing your business model in some way—either by changing the commercial model or the way you generate business or fulfill orders. This is optimization, and very few companies are actually at this stage. Based on anecdotal evidence, I would suggest that 60 percent of all businesses are still getting the interface right, and about 30 percent have moved to the data stage. Only about 10 percent at best are at the optimization level. When people talk about digital transformation—this is the promised land.

Optimization can take many forms—in it turns out that Airbnb didn't just disrupt hotels, it also disrupted the home rental market. In France, which is the second largest market for Airbnb, the data suggests that it pushes rents up in places such as Paris and Marseille. For Airbnb, renting entire homes for short leases has become a more powerful approach compared to just a spare room. Optimization may be just a minor tweak—such as a utility company changing a route for its service van, or it could end up as a significant rethink of the business model, such as a coffee shop charging for time spent in its Wi-Fi-enabled store, and giving the coffee away for free. Each business and industry will have its own patterns for optimization, based on context, current inefficiencies, and opportunities. Optimization is optional—you may just be happy with the first two stages, but it is highly improbable that the higher visibility and data offer no opportunities for improving your business.

The Rise of RPA

It would be fair to say that the past three centuries of industrialization have largely been about three layers of automation. The first was a shift from manual to steam power—of ploughs, looms, and locomotives. The second was a shift from steam to electricity. And the third, in the second half of the 20th century, was about a shift to computerization. While the first two were all about the source of energy, the third was about management. Not just of the machines, but also of the processes, both in the factories and in the offices created by the first two stages of industrialization.

Today, we take automation for granted. From the coffee machine in my kitchen, to the ATM where I get cash, and from the contactless credit card I use to pay for my train ticket, to the way my travel expenses get reimbursed. There's automation all around us. Even while I type this, a copy of this document is being stored on a cloud using a behind-the-scenes automation. The role of automation in our lives is reflected in its prominence popular culture as well. Charles Chaplin gets entangled with the machine in *Modern Times* (1936). Ferris Bueller (1986) automates his dummy in the eponymous movie. And even in the animation film *Sing* (2016), Rosita automates her family's morning routine from breakfast to school departure, with ultimately calamitous impact!

A dark side of process consistency is that it has reduced humans to robotic beings, devoid of any intellectual contribution to their job, and reduced to following a tightly defined script or instruction. In fact, that reason that so many jobs in factories and offices have already been automated is that they were jobs that had been broken down into a level that could be addressed by subhuman intelligence. From the number of minutes that potatoes must be fried, to the number of rings of a phone call before it needs to be answered. Every company depends on process adherence driven by consistency and repeatability. The industrial era had already thus reduced humans to machines, so replacing them by other machines was relatively simple, and had the added benefits that computers and machines don't get tired or bored, and their output isn't impacted by their emotional state. But this meant that only those processes where judgment was removed, that is, had been robotized, could be automated—such as fast food preparation or call center responses.

A lot of processes in the previous generation of automation involved getting people to enter data into systems. But this also resulted in multiple and often unconnected systems and data islands. A single process could span these systems and involve a manual data input from one system to the other. When businesses look at their financial cycles such as order to cash, or procure to pay, these manual points represent inefficiencies and sources of errors. Robotic process automation (RPA) systems create *robots* that can automate this by mimicking the steps followed by the human process. These narrow, software robots are designed to only perform one task. For example, get your accounts receivable information into your CRM system.

Doing this under the hood, or via an API, may be expensive and time-consuming. The category of tools broadly known as RPA looks to solve this process-level automation and optimization problem. They still use programmatic tools, but they mimic the human act of extracting from one system and entering into another. This is done through software *robots,* which are designed for individual processes and keep working away to run the process as a human should. Although the business case for RPA is often built around reduction of people, the reality is that it enables people to be freed from rote and repeated data entry tasks for more rewarding work. But it is also true that over time, this makes the overall business process more flexible. RPA tools have attracted huge investments of late. UI Path, one of the three major providers, had an IPO in 2021, which valued the company at $29bn. A number of new players are now in the fray, coming in from different software segments such as CRM, middleware, and AI, attracted by the high growth in this segment. According to some reports, automation was the fastest growing area of enterprise software in 2020, which is not surprising, given that a typical large organization deploys upward of 150 to 175 applications, and many processes require interactions with a significant cross-section of these apps.

Tip: Think of any job that requires the reduction of human judgment in favor of a predefined set of steps and ask yourself why we need humans to do this job instead of machines.

There are also processes that have never been automated because they have worked off physical documents or handwritten forms. These may have originated outside your organization—for example, bills of loading for cargo, or diagnostic lab reports for health insurance companies. Increasingly, RPA products are able to offer digitizing processes involving these kinds of documents on the back of character recognition, or even handwriting recognition. Additionally, there are libraries of industry terms that are recognized by the software platforms, so if you're looking at medical compliance information, the software will be able to recognize abbreviations, terms, or even logos related to compliance bodies. Today's technology can therefore do more, and automate more complex tasks—such as grammar and spell-checking documents, recognizing a song and matching the lyrics to the music, or checking expense claims, where the instructions can't be codified into a set of sequential tasks. This is often referred to as intelligent process automation (IPA) and is a natural evolution of the RPA model.

The Future of Automation

One of the fascinating aspects of robotic automation is the implication for the workplace and HR. As more rote jobs are picked up by software, systems, and robots, humans are no longer performing those jobs and are instead presumably doing more creative work, or work involving more judgment or higher order skills. But that also requires rethinking of metrics and goals. HR organizations may need to rethink job descriptions, training and reskilling, and measurement—how roles and performance are measured in this world of co-bots (colleagues who are also robots). The optimization of processes may therefore also lead to an optimization of HR.

A useful way of thinking about automation over the next few years is that previous generations of automation involved systems that required humans to be trained to operate them. In the emergent digital world, the systems use machines that are trained to work with humans.

The Productivity Paradox

There is a strong correlation between the size of organizations and the amount of time wasted within its walls. Try this exercise. When you go for lunch with another person rather than just by yourself, you will invariably add a few minutes agreeing when and where to go, and just when you're ready, the other person will be finishing a call. Now try with three, four, and five people, and watch the coordination time shoot up exponentially, till you simply have to name the place and time and ask whoever wants in to be there.

It's not just at lunchtime though. In large companies, time is wasted in a vast variety of ways and at an industrial scale. E-mail is one of the big culprits, but so are internal admin and the never-ending drive toward faux efficiency. Many organizations will save headcount and the cost footprint of the IT department, the travel desk, and other back office operations, but nobody counts the hours wasted by employees on systems that don't work. Perhaps because decision makers in large traditional environments often have assistants doing much of their administrative work, and don't feel the pain themselves!

Being insensitive to employee time makes your business less efficient, it impacts culture and retention of talent, and it promotes shadow IT— where your people use their own digital tools, leading to compromises in your information security. Companies, such as KDS (now the Neo Technology Group), provide systems through which you can book travel and complete expenses in minutes, with minimal manual work. I have seen this solution elicit an almost emotional response from people in large companies, who have to spend hours over these administrative tasks.

Remember that, thanks to our personal digital tools, we've learned to value every five minutes because it can be productively used. Most people are trying to fit in as much as they can into one life. Why wouldn't you give them the tools to do as much as they can for their job?

The New Productivity

When we talk about productivity in industrial and economic terms, we usually implicitly mean labor productivity. Typically measured in terms of the output per individual. And there has been a concern that over the past

decades, despite all the influx of technology and computing, labor productivity, or output per employee hasn't really shifted much. From where
we stand, this may actually be asking the wrong question. Ford produced
over six million cars, in 2007, and a similar number in 2020, but it has
done so with 40 percent less people, from 300,000 to 185,000 in that
time. Note that technology that makes people more efficient is different
from technology that replaces people. In the case of the latter, the simpli-
fied measure of labor productivity is no longer valid. Capital now consti-
tutes an increasingly larger part of the value of a typical product. Often
therefore, investment decisions are made on the basis of how to make
the machines more productive, rather than the people. The battleground
has shifted to the return on capital. While labor productivity remains an
important metric for the government, the landscape for investment may
have shifted.

Robots

*When Isaac Asimov was born in Petrovichi, in Russia, the Czech author
Karel Capek was publishing his science fiction play Rossumovi Univerzální
Roboti (R.U.R.)—the play that would give the world the concept of a
"Robot." Ironically enough, when Asimov's family made the journey of
almost 7,500 km to Brooklyn New York, three years later, Capek's play was
also crossing the Atlantic to be screened in the United States as Rossum's
Universal Robots. Asimov went on to become one of the great thinkers
about robots—constructing the three famous laws.*

In a way, this all seems very ordained. But let's remind ourselves that robots
were intended as *workers* who would perform tasks. They would be powered by computers, so their capability was circumscribed by the processing
power of the computers of the day. As we move into the world of hyper-
intelligent computers, including all forms of AI, robots will continue to
grow in capability. As such, robots fall into the realm of automation. They
are designed for performing physical tasks that humans can't or don't want
to do. Carry things, fix things, lift things. Any number of manufacturing
processes are not run by robots–a significant part of car is built by them.

The robots conceived by Asimov were actually an amalgam of a number of distinct ideas. The first is a physical, humanoid form, which would enable the anthropomorphism of robots. The second is an AI-like brain, which could power the robot and enable it to perform tasks. The third is the range of tasks the robot can perform—starting with specific narrow physical tasks, to rote processing work, through to more sophisticated *intelligent* work. In parallel, the interface or communication could evolve from very basic and specific commands to natural language and voice-based commands. The path to this humanoid version of robots is circuitous, and the progress is, to quote William Gibson, "unevenly distributed." We have made a lot of progress in narrow tasks performed by robots. These range from physical tasks performed by physical robots—such as automobile manufacturing, to processing tasks performed by software robots, which have no physical presence. Both however are examples of automation—which is essentially the act of replacing a human performed process with a software and/or hardware. Usually resulting in less errors, more precision, efficient scaling, and crucially more transparency and data.

As each task is picked up by a robot, or a machine, that is electronic rather than mechanical, it creates a new source of data. The benefit of automation is immediate, but the benefit of this new interface and data is arguably larger over the long term. As with any interface, it starts to give us an ability to improve the performance of the machine and therefore of the process itself. The interface is between the robot and its environment, or its task. But it is equally an interface between the organization and its environment.

The idea of robots as quasi-sentient beings is covered extensively in science fiction. Two that deserve mention are: *2001 A Space Odyssey* (cocreated by Arthur C Clarke and Stanley Kubric in 1968) and *I, Robot* (written in the 1940s by Asimov, and turned into a film by Alex Proyas in 2004). Both explore the notion of a powerful and thinking computer that goes beyond its brief to take decisions that are contradictory to its stated purpose and with potentially deleterious and far-reaching effects. But the very idea of a thinking robot or machine is the realm of artificial intelligence, which we shouldn't confuse with the notion of automation. Think of it as the brain versus the body. In the world of automation—be it a robot, a piece of software, or a machine, we are simply building a tool to perform tasks. The task robot can do nothing more than the tasks it is explicitly designed for. And as such, it is simply another interface that will generate data for the brain. To understand how we are looking to supplement the brain, read the chapter on AI.

The word robot is used loosely and to mean a number of different things today. One way of classifying robots is as hardware (having some physical form) and software robots. A robot may be an arm connected to a machine that can lift pallets and stack them. Or something that automatically fixes caps on bottles. The question is, what makes these different from traditional machines? Why is something a robot and not just an extractor, or a press? Likewise, software robots automate tasks such as completing workflows or processing documents or images. The same question may be asked—why is it a robot and not just software? The answer to both of these questions lies in how we classify automation. Task automation is done by traditional machines or software. They are narrow in their focus and can do one thing with little or no freedom. Usually, when we mean process automation, we are referring to a series of one or more tasks that cumulatively achieve a goal. The focus is very much on the goal rather than the task. While any machine or software can focus on a task it's given and perform that task repetitively (like fixing hinges to doors or vacuum sealing bottles), when we refer to robots, we are usually referring to the achievement of goals that may involve more than one task. Often there is some basic decision making involved, and elements of higher-level processing and even bits of AI may be involved. Any process automation involves some level of basic decision making. For example, the Roomba automated vacuum cleaner, or Gita the carrier robot. Both of these can scan the environment using a range of technologies, take a number of decisions but ultimately are focused on completing a job that they are assigned.

Tip: See the YouTube videos from Boston Dynamics (now a part of Hyundai) to understand the power of what robots can do, and also how they could be nonhumanoid.

CHAPTER 24

Optimizing Health Care

Growing up in Kolkata, India—we had a family pediatrician, a family GP, and a few specialists that we knew and trusted. Moreover, doctors were always found through recommendations—the whole health care system seemed to be a large social network. While on the one hand, it had little or no computerization to speak of, there was nonetheless a lot of retention of data because of the longevity of the relationships and the semisocial nature of the arrangements. For instance, when you went to your doctor for say a problem, he would remember instantly that you were diabetic, had a kidney stone removed a year ago, and were allergic to penicillin. This was fine, until you moved cities and had to start all over again. This is still how a lot of health care works in many parts of the world. The poor laborer on a building site has no social connections to good doctors and is reliant on a ramshackle public infrastructure, and there is no universal insurance or social security. This is being tackled at a number of levels, but at the core of these is the ability to handle data. When there is no data retention via relationships or systems, only the fortunate few can get the appropriate quality of health care. The situation for countries like India is exacerbated due to the size of population and the economic constraints.

Conversely, the NHS in the UK was underpinned by a vision and execution that outstripped many other countries, for decades. Of late, the structural, political and operational complexity of the NHS and its funding process has become a barrier to innovation. One of the most obvious areas where you could see this work was in terms of data—every visit to a doctor often required you to start all over again. This is changing as we speak, as electronic patient records are being adopted at scale.

Public health care in the UK covers 89 percent of the population, and even for the remaining 11 percent, it provides accident and emergency, mental health, and other services.[1] Public health care spending in the UK grew steadily till 2009 but has been stagnant at about £130bn.

The estimated funding shortfall was anticipated to increase to between £16bn and £30bn by 2020/2021,[2] even before COVID-19 and related expenses hit the budget. Thanks to improved health care, people continue to live longer in each generation, ironically shackling the health care system into funding shortfall and debt. It is quite likely that the retirement age will also creep up, but the ratio of working to nonworking people will still rise. This poses a ticking time bomb of a problem—not just financially, but operationally as well. Future governments will not have the budgets to simply solve by spending more, and nor will they have access to the skills and people needed. There is a pressing need for innovation in how the same level or better health care can be delivered with ever lower budgets. Technology will almost certainly be required to bridge this gap in the UK, as with many European nations with public health care funding. The COVID-19 pandemic, which disproportionately impacted older people, was a harsh reminder of how exposed the health care systems are to shocks.

The United States spends more per capita on health care than any other country but still has a lower life expectancy than most European countries. There have been many papers and articles published on this, but it is also true that health care is unevenly distributed in the United States. And even basic health care is a high cost service that many people can't afford. Health care, coupled with aging populations, is therefore a universal problem, and digital tools and optimization are not an option any more.

Connected Health

Technology intervention in health care takes many forms. It includes smartphones and apps for patients, wearables for fitness, use of AI for anticipating secondary infections, fundamental changes in medicine driven through bio-electrical methods, phantomization of health care, shift of focus to population health and prevention over cure, use of video to connect patients to experts, overcoming disabilities through assistive tech, 3D printing of prosthetics, and many others. In fact, many of these are already in place. I believe that the 2020s will be the decade of health care innovation.

As with most things digital, the initial focus of digital health care will involve a surge in connections. This process has already begun, and we see examples of this all around us already. Here are some examples you may have seen.

Fitness tracking wearables: in 2020, just under 450 million wearable devices were shipped across the world. If you have witnessed friends and relatives being anxious to complete their 10,000 steps for the day, or perhaps are yourself, you've seen the influence of wearable fitness devices. This already extends to other consumer health devices—including blood pressure and blood sugar monitors, and weighing scales, which are increasingly smart and connected, with reminder services that encourage you to be regular with your daily check-in.[3] Waire, a Scotland-based startup offers a single device to be worn with a strap on the arm, which will offer cuffless blood pressure estimation, respiration rate, temperature, oxygen saturation, three-axis position, motion, ECG, heart rate, and more.[4] Virtual and video checkups are now regularly used in the United States,[5] and the pandemic has also made this a worldwide phenomenon.

All of these improve the efficiency of the system as well as patient experience, for example, getting patients to be monitored more effectively and regularly, or getting patients to speak with specialists faster. Digital solutions are also usually lower cost and more self-service-oriented, which creates more ownership of individual health and more compliance and awareness, generally lowering the rate of admissions and readmissions. But all of this is only the first step, and even that is not complete. We are not yet in a world where we've connected the patient to the care ecosystem. As more and more connections are created in the health care space, the more data we'll generate and how we deal with the data will drive the second level of improvements.

Quantifying and Optimizing Health Care

Nurses working in hospitals in Ireland might complete up to 72 tasks in an hour. But they constantly work on an interruptive rather than scheduled basis. This means that they are constantly interrupted by patient needs. This can lead to nurses missing signals, or tracking changes in vital signs across multiple patients. Syncrophi,[6] an award-winning software, connects all the existing medical systems to create a single dashboard with a supervised queue system. The nurses work on a risk score and decisions are based on this, but in the high-pressure environment, there can be up to a 50 percent chance of error—ranging from adding mistakes to data entry errors on multiple systems. The KEWS system from Syncrophi connects all the individual systems and creates a single queue of tasks, which are being reordered through the day as the patients' conditions and needs change. The continuous quantification of risks ensures that nurses can focus on their tasks and also retain a view across an entire ward or a whole hospital.

Acute kidney infection (AKI) is hard to predict and can escalate quickly. It's a key risk for people already undergoing a major operation or treatment. DeepMind, an Alphabet subsidiary, analyzes multiple streams of patient data to calculate the risk of AKI. In the Royal Free Hospital in London, clinicians use DeepMind as a warning system[7] in order to prevent or plan for the onset of AKI in a patent. Data sharing concerns notwithstanding, this is a very good example of the levels of optimization that the health care industry will be reaching for in future.

Healthy aging is another critical area, given the demographic profile of many European nations. Japan has already gone down this path, with the United States likely to follow Europe. Today, a number of providers are setting up homes with sensors so that activities of daily living can be tracked. The idea is that the data this generates creates a complete picture of the habits and lifestyles of the resident. Also, once this has been running, it can catch any deviations from regular patterns, such as not waking up at the normal time, or an increase in the use of the toilet, or disturbed sleep, and so on. These can be early pointers for the onset of specific conditions, or alerts can be set up for carers or family members to check in when there is unexpected data or movement. Ultimately, this changes the way that care is planned and delivered, with remote monitoring of data playing a key role in the mix. TCS has piloted this kind of solution in Singapore and Ireland.

Similarly, the use of electronic patient records at large scale allows the focus on population health. This includes measures to keep people out of hospital, control epidemics, track the growth of specific diseases, and more. The optimization of health care involves less, rather than more health care. But this can only happen when patients are connected and their data is quantified. The CEO of Waire recently pointed out to me that we track our automobiles more diligently than we track our own body and health. I believe we're on the cusp of not only changing how we track and monitor, but how we quantify and optimize health care.

Tip: Make a mental list of what data you actually capture and track about your own health unless you have a specific diagnosed problem.

CHAPTER 25

Optimizing Customer Experience

Here's a conundrum for you. Regis McKenna wrote an excellent piece in the *Harvard Business Review* in 1991 called *Marketing is Everything*. He argued that marketing was not just the task of attracting the customers to your product or brand, but that in a customer-centric world, marketing was the touchstone for the whole business. The principles around every part of business should operate. Yet, in 2017, another article in the same publication, called *Why CMOs Never Last* by Whitler and Morgan shared data on the tenure of chief marketing officers have been steadily declining. Another recent trend is the rise of chief customer officers (CCO), whose remit extends to the full cycle of customer experience. CCOs are supplanting CMOs. Their reach includes what was once the purview of operations. Marketing has indeed become everything and nothing.

The New Customer

Digital era customers behaviors have not only changed, they have also morphed quickly with new technologies, platforms, and trends. Customers have grown much more fickle—brand loyalty has dropped, and their behaviors have splintered and shifted. They block or skip through ads. They *cut the cord* and binge watch OTT channels. They demanded instant gratification and 24/7 availability. And they don't conform to the traditional segmentation rules. But an ever-larger proportion of the new customers behaviors is already connected and quantified. Knowingly or unknowingly, consumers are also optimizing their lives around digital tools. Here are some of the new digital behaviors that you need to optimize for.

The Encyclopedia Effect: The Consumer Knows More

When a consumer walks into a TV showroom today, the smart money is on the probability that she knows more about the product than the person behind the counter. It's not just about TVs, consumers today have all the means and are in the habit of thoroughly researching their purchase—including features, price comparisons, technologies, accessories, and performance. They are also armed with opinions of friends via social media, as well as in store comparisons via mobile devices. This calls for an entirely new way of assisting informed customers make their choices effectively, rather than old mode of handholding or even nudging buyers into choices.

The Shazam Effect: Telescoping AIDA

Back then (more than 15 years ago), you heard a song, you tried to find out what it was, maybe you heard it again, then on the radio. Somebody told you what the song was if you were able to hum it. Or you searched the lyrics on the Internet. You went to the music store/Amazon and bought the cd, if it was worth the £16.99, or whatever the arbitrary price point for the cd was. Now you hear and like a song that you've never heard before, you *Shazam* or SoundCloud it, and it tells you the song, artist, and offers you the chance to buy it with a single click of iTunes. In 30 seconds, from never having heard the song, you now own it. This telescoping of the traditional *AIDA* marketing and sales cycle is seen across categories and consumers are expecting it. If you run out of toothpaste, it can be ordered from Amazon in seconds. You will soon be able to upload a picture of a dress and get a search result for similar if not exact garments as well as retail stores in proximity or delivery options. Real time is in. Waiting is out. How real time is your business?

The Interface Is Dead: Long Live the Interface

We've been through multiscreens, second-screens, and even third screens, but what is happening now is much more amorphous. The screen is vanishing, yet it's everywhere. On your watch, in your line of sight from a wearable frame, on your shoes, and in your car. In fact, sometimes it's not a screen at all, just a natural interface. Think of Nest, or Amazon Echo, and it's not a screen that comes to mind, is it? And once we get into the IOT, the environment will be one giant interface. With both computing and interfaces becoming much more amorphous, you and your consumer will always be connected in multiple ways. Are you ready for this kind of commitment?

Fragmented Identities

What's even more granular than the individual? Federated identities. Your customer in her office and the same customer at the park with her kids are not really the same persona. Her needs are different, different receptors are being used, and her emotional states are different. In the pre-digital world, it would have been near-impossible to tailor messaging to this kind of contextual personas, which are segments of an individual. But today, the customer can signal her intent based on the profile she explicitly chooses on her device.

Attention Deficiency

First there were letters, then came e-mails, then text messages, and Twitter. Our patience for longer communication has dwindled both as senders and receivers. Newspapers and long op-eds have given way to snappy blogs and bullet point memos. Videos have replaced text, and short videos have replaced the longer formats. TikTok is now a *unicorn* (a startup with a billion dollar valuation). You get the gist—we are increasingly in an attention starved economy. Attention is fragmented, fleeting, and in generally very short supply. Meanwhile, the volume of noise keeps going up, so finding the signal becomes even harder. What little attention consumers have, they guard ever more zealously. How ready are you for micro-engagements and micro-transactions?

Trust Erosion

Who do we trust? Not the government, not large enterprises, not banks or telcos, and not Google or Facebook. Yet, we trust the feedback of strangers on recommendation websites. However, you still wouldn't trust a random stranger to provide you with broadband services, find stuff on the Internet quickly, or hold your savings for you. Trust can mean competence or ethical alignment. You would still trust the bank with your money because they have demonstrable competence, and because they are regulated. Trust is the basic currency of all communication, and consequently, for brand creation. Organizations use trust mechanisms to very you as a customer. Blockchains are federating and tokenizing trust and creating a completely different way to transact on trust, via the network.

Three New Models for Customer Experience

Getting to True Omnichannel

I don't believe I've met a bank or a retailer in the past five years who don't have an omnichannel initiative on. The omnichannel initiatives have the additional objective of integrating the customer experience across channels, and allowing users to alternate between channels as they wish. You should be able to start a search on the website, call the company with some queries, and finally, conclude the transaction on your mobile device or in person. And at each of these points, the company should be able to continue the conversation from where you left off on the previous channel. In order to do this, every channel needs to be connected and quantified. Even physical store visits can be digitized if you can incentivize customers to be recognized via their mobile devices when they are in the store. Once every channel is connected and quantified, you can do interesting optimizations. Tesco famously allowed shoppers to use images of products at train stations to add items to their shopping basket. But you could have all kinds of combinations. Shop on the bus, pick up at store, shop in the aisle on the way to a movie, and get it delivered with the ecommerce order and so on.

Lifetime Models

Everybody wants customers to come back to for future purchases—be they upgrades, replacements, or just continuing to buy more products as they need them. If you're an insurance company, for example, you know that one of the first types of insurance that people buy is usually car insurance when they start driving. A typical consumer may subsequently buy health insurance for himself when he starts work, or professional insurance if he starts a business. He may purchase family cover when he gets married, and home insurance when he starts a family. This kind of pattern driven by life stages and key life events is a simple model that an insurance company might construct toward creating a lifetime model of a customer. Such a model should be a staple of health care and education businesses that are likely to have a lifelong association with a customer. But equally for banks, credit cards, retailers, and even restaurants. Within the limits of data privacy principles, there's no reason why every customer shouldn't be a customer for life, assuming they're happy with your service.

Life Cycle Models

This brings us to another important redefinition of marketing and digital. Companies still focus their efforts on acquisition rather than retention of customers.[1] This is true of digital expenditures and also of the focus of marketing. Yet, as we've just discussed, customer experience (i.e. of existing customers) is historically not owned by the marketing function—it is much more impacted by the decisions of the COO or the CFO—in the way that the delivery of services and the support systems work. It is now part of marketing lore that selling to new customers cost much more than existing ones. Yet, retention is often the black hole of the digital experience. Historically, industries where switching between providers is time- and effort-intensive, customers have often been taken for granted but with most industries now offering easy switching, thanks to regulation, the time may have come to give digital pride of place in the battle for retention. This means customer centricity, understanding journeys and pain points, and the use of digital tools and data to make it as easy as possible for customers to buy and consume new services, as to fix problems. Especially as your products become connected and intelligent, and allow you to access usage data.

Tip: Observe a 13 to 14-year-old in your family and find out how they use digital products—look for completely different ways of using devices or tools from what you're expecting to see.

CHAPTER 26

Optimizing the Workplace

Optimized Meetings?

You've probably heard it mentioned that the pandemic has accelerated the journey to digital transformation. One of the areas where this has played out in interesting ways is in the idea of the workplace. Initially, when most of us were working from home, meetings switched almost completely to online meetings on tools such as Teams and Zoom. This took some getting used to, and a steep learning curve for some. But online meetings offer have some advantages that are worth exploring. After all, an online meeting is nothing but a *connected* meeting. Which means that we can move quickly to the quantification phase. What is a quantified meeting? Well, that depends on what you want to measure. Presumably, a good meeting is one where everybody is heard, conversations are productive. Decisions are made. Actions are agreed and assigned. Or a combination of all of these. And all of this is done as efficiently as possible. These things are quite hard to measure in real-world meetings. Although you always know when a meeting wasn't great, which can happen for any number of reasons: somebody hogged the conversation, attendees were underprepared, no actions were agreed, or an item not on the agenda ended up taking most of the time.

Thanks to the need to stay competitive, the providers of online meeting tools have been innovating at pace over the past months. So, you can actually get a transcript of a Teams meeting, or record the entire meeting. And it is also possible to report on the percentage of airtime taken by each participant. Applying some machine learning tools, it would also be possible to extract from the transcript whether or not any actions were agreed, who they were assigned to, and if dates were agreed. Was the agenda covered? Was the meeting constructive or disruptive? And armed with this information, could you re-design your meetings? Amazon famously eschews PowerPoint presentations in its internal meetings in favor of a memo that everybody needs to spend the first few minutes reading. But this is driven by Jeff Bezos's vision. And while it's worked for Amazon, this is not to say this is right for everybody, or that it can't be improved on. If you could actually see the data from your meetings, there's no doubt you'd see many ways to improve the time spent.

As we come out of the pandemic, we're going to be in a hybrid world. Partly online, partly offline. Nobody quite knows the exact shape of the hybrid work, and the balance may vary with companies, jobs, individual preferences, cultures, and so on. Everybody seems to agree that the reason for going into work is not to sit at a desk, but to meet colleagues formally and informally, and get more *face-to-face* time. Ironically, online meetings, which are already connected and quantified, may be much more effective in many ways. Can we find ways to bring this into the real world? You could have a voice assistant in physical meetings—think of an Alexa or Siri-like device as one of your meeting participants, which is taking notes, recording the conversation, and providing exactly the same analysis as we outlined for online meetings. It would be the same as actually having a dedicated observer for each meeting tasked to evaluate meetings, raise a flag if the conversation is digressing, and report back on the quality of the meeting.

IT Is the New HR

How do you interact with your bank? Digital, undoubtedly! How do you buy books? Talk to your friends? Engage with the government—increasingly digital, right? Talk to hotels, train companies, and airlines for your holidays? Find a date? Order pizza? Catch the latest news? Listen to music? Watch your favorite TV show? The chances are that you do all of this digitally. Not only that each of these processes have been digitized, fine-tuned, turned into easy-to-use apps, and optimized over time so that they are highly friction-free experiences. You can book a return train ticket and a hotel for a night of stay for a trip to Manchester, from London, in under five minutes. This is the digital experience we're all used to, today.

The employee experience is still catching up with this. Thanks to cloud-based enterprise applications, single sign-on, collaboration tools such as Teams, Slack, or Google, or even Facebook@Work, things are improving every day. Which begs the question, in a digital world, what defines the impression that your employees and colleagues carry about the organization? And how is this manifested? Historically, your HR organization would own this, through the entire journey of an employee—hiring, onboarding, performance management, career architectures and exits, and spanning working conditions, morale, productivity, and satisfaction. My belief is that in a digital and connected organization, it is in fact your digital experience that drives all of this. Whatever the policies defined by IT, they are manifested in the way your digital tooling delivers them to employees. Your company may have a principle of being employee-friendly. But unless your digital interface is able to deliver on this promise, it will remain unfulfilled. This is why I say that IT is the new HR in the digital world. Not because your IT organization defines your leave policy. But they often deliver the experience that defines your view of the organization.

Starting Early

A few months ago, in a conversation with my HR colleagues, we chanced upon the fact that preboarding experience for every other organization we know is an experience that can be improved. Typically, from the time you accept an offer of employment from an organization, you are a virtual employee. Over the next few weeks and months, you will be anticipating your new joining experiences, wondering about your new colleagues, and planning for being effective as soon as you join. During this time, you will receive many requests for referral information, bank details, personal details, and be asked to fill a number of forms. But invariably, you don't know how many activities or steps are still left to go, and what's going in in your new organization on a day-to-day basis. In order to fix this, we built an app working with a very smart start up called Blink. Blink's app is designed to work with remote employees. Our idea was to treat new joiners as remote employees, and overlay the Blink app with features designed for new joiners. We gamified the joining process with clarity about the total number of steps, broken into levels. Prospective employees get rewarded for completing each step, can provide feedback, can post questions, seek clarifications, and connect with fellow joiners on a common platform. But the immediate benefit of this is that the HR team can see in a single dashboard the status of all new joiners, what percentage of tasks have been completed, and whether any key milestone is missing. We've immediately connected and quantified the preboarding process. Optimization will invariably follow as the data will tell us where the preboarding process for any organization is performing well, or badly, and where new joiners are getting a poor experience even before they've joined their new organization.

PART 6

Summary and Conclusion

As you've probably seen by now, almost any industry can be digitally optimized. Here are a couple of examples.

Salman Khan of the Khan academy wants to do optimize education. He wants children to learn on a digital platform in their own time and at their own speed. In his inverted view of education, the classroom is where children come to review, discuss, and get special attention from teachers on areas where they need help. Because the teacher can see on the platform what the student did and what they struggled with. The students' performance on the platform is already quantified.

Pathadisha (which means directions for travel) is a very interesting startup I met, which connects all modes of public transport in Kolkata, India, and also tracks users' data via their smartphones. Consumers can track arrival times at bus stops for any of 18,000 individual buses by route number for example. But collectively, by pulling all of this data together, Pathadisha gives you a snapshot of ferries, trams, buses, subway, and trains, all plying in the city. This is being used by the local authorities to schedule transport better and by private providers to assess when surges in demand might occur. Pathadisha is optimizing public transport and was even used to manage temporary travel passes on the Kolkata Metro (subway) during COVID-19 restrictions.[1]

The Big Trends

You will have picked up a few common patterns through the book. Let's look at some of these big trends, which are germane to every industry. Interfaces are continuously evolving—from mobiles, to sensors, to nanotechnology inside our bodies, to chatbots on websites, to voice and natural language, and even to brain signals. Service design frameworks are critical to getting users to adopt these interfaces.

The stream of data from this universal connectivity explodes into a tsunami of data. The continuously falling cost of storage, better tools, and frameworks for dealing with data and improved analytical frameworks and AI both address and encourage this explosive growth of data. For businesses, the worlds of operational data, customer data, environmental data, and enterprise data merge into a single ocean of usable information. The successful future organization will be a data-centric organization, but we are still to understand what that means in terms of structures, practices, and processes. Certainly, data protection and ethics will take center stage.

Work gets smarter—we are freed from the shackles of office desks and working hours, and new ways of measuring work will evolve. Processes will get atomized. Company boundaries will blur, as well industry definitions. This evolution of work will have huge societal implications. We will need to address the many challenges if we want to reap the benefits of a postindustrial phase.

Businesses will need to be architected for change. Not like transformer toys, which can be one of just two things, but like Lego sets, which can be rearranged repeatedly, quickly, and effectively. Cloud enablement, and moving to the *Enterprise as a service*, coupled with strong API layer management and smart security will be the levers of this change architecture. A lot of organizations will have to frequently restructure and reorganize, but the winners will be those who can control this better and do so quickly. Those that take months for new structures to start making sense will suffer.

Single, monopolistic markets will abound, especially in the digital component of any industry. The scale-free network pattern will drive ecommerce, media, and other industries to this highly skewed model, of winners take all. Regulation will be one of the primary barriers to this monopolistic trends—whether it is regional such as in China, or global as in the case of banks.

Disintermediation and platformization will continue to create and disrupt industries. Efficiencies will be found and removed via platforms and removal of nonvalue-added intermediaries. Providers and creators will be connected more directly to consumers. The successful dis-intermediaries will be platforms such as TripAdvisor or Spotify, rather than resellers or aggregators such as traditional travel agents or record labels.

We will see two kinds of automation—task and process automation, and decision and outcome automation. Task and process automation will typically be done by software and hardware systems that are often described as robotic. These will work within specific boundaries and have a relatively narrow set of functions and conditions under which they work. Cars are being built in robotic factories and a lot of manual processing is being replaced by robotic process automation (RPA) software. On the other hand, decision automation tools powered by AI will start to replace much more advanced work—such as driving cars and managerial roles, even creative ones. AI is clearly a mega trend and could take us into the realm of singularity.

All of this will happen in increasingly smarter and networked environments. The energy network, transport network, and our homes and offices will all be able to share data, and smart devices and processes will feed off that data. Your electric car left overnight to charge will negotiate with the smart grid to agree the best rate and time to charge, thereby giving you the best deal and also allowing the grid to load balance. Our decision models will be significantly more capable of understanding and exploiting network effects rather than just individual behaviors. For example, methods for fighting crime or fraud, and addressing mental health and other health care problems could be significantly improved by the increased modeling of network effects.

All of these changes will place a huge responsibility on the leadership of organizations at all levels. Leaders will need to combine the ability to manage design, technology, and business, appreciate regulatory impact, and continuously craft and update their vision of the world today and tomorrow, and be able recalibrate this journey, and their organizations. The drive to becoming a data-centric organization should become one of the most critical tasks of leaders. Correspondingly, there needs to be a significant re-education process in the board room around data, risk, security, and the accelerating change.

The Conceptual Digital Framework

I've always found it useful to structure digital thinking into the layers— technology (interfaces and digital infrastructure), design, data, and analytics. This protects us from confusing and overlapping concepts. Sometimes even one *system* such as an app on a phone can be broken up into these three layers—especially if this represents a service such as a bank or streaming music. Each of these layers comprises many different technologies, which are all evolving at varying paces. Design thinking is the critical differentiator between the adoption or rejection of new technologies.

Automation, robotics, or AI systems are by themselves categories of systems that have all these layers. We also need to consider that the next generation of digital technologies will merge the digital and physical worlds as never before, so those of us who have grown up distinguishing between the *real world* and the *digital world* will have to reorient ourselves all over again.

The Future Is Not More of the Past

Despite the vast and sweeping changes that we've seen so far, in the past three decades, it's sobering to think that we may in future think of this period as one of glacially slow progress. I've pointed to two specific points— that is, the invention of HTML (which led to the birth of the World Wide Web) and the creation of the smartphone as key points of inflexion. In future, these points may happen more frequently, or there may be a much more diffused and continuous set of inventions and discoveries that drive us forward faster than ever. Exponential change is all around us.

Transformation is clearly a huge underlying theme here. The role of technologists may go from building and operating technology, to driving organizational architecture and governance, and having the data stewardship in connection with the data and security officers. In all this, the need to handle exponential change while retaining resilience will still rest with the leadership and the board.

How Do We Make It Work?

Our simple methodology, therefore, which calls itself connect, quantify, optimize is a really an adaptation of the basic scientific method. Whereas, in a scientific experiment, you might need to gather data explicitly, digital by its nature allows us to gather the data out of the very interaction of the user with the technology. The analysis of this data can lead to a restatement of the whole business premise—known in the startup world as a *pivot*, or it can be a marginal tweak to the solution to make it a little bit more effective. This cycle of *connect, quantify, optimize*, or to restate it: *try, learn, evolve* can be done very quickly and efficiently with the right tools and skills in the digital space. But it can grow rapidly to redefine large global corporations as well.

Let me end with a story. One morning about three years ago, we came downstairs to discover that our car had been stolen. Our neighbor's CCTV footage showed a couple of men getting into the car and driving it away at 4 AM. As it happens, just the same week, we had signed up for a new insurance for the car, which involved putting a tracking device on the car and using the data to rate our driving and give us a better quote. We promptly called the insurance company to report the stolen car but also to tell them to track it using the device they had put in. The first response was that the telematics team has a 14-day response SLA. Then we were told it was outsourced to a different company. Later in the day, thanks to my wife's persistence, it emerged that it wasn't a separate company but a different division. From Friday morning, till Monday, we pestered the insurer until at 9:30 AM on Monday we got through to the telematics team. Who took 30 seconds to tell us exactly where our car was. We spent all of Monday staking out our own car until the police arrived to take over, and our car was finally recovered safe and sound.

What's really interesting is that neither the insurance provider nor the police thought of the tracker as the obvious and immediate option. We were actually covered for the cost of the car, so the loss would have been the insurers. No matter how great your technology is, unless you reshape your operations around it, you won't get anywhere near the full benefit from it.

That's really the bottom line to this book. Technology evolution is fundamental. Design thinking is crucial, and data and analysis are essential for digital change and success. But none of them by themselves is sufficient. Combining them and redefining the way you work, or even what business you run, is the only way you'll succeed, or perhaps even survive in the digital age.

Notes

Chapter 1

1. *Gajar ka Halwa*—An Indian carrot based dessert.
2. Amazon patent for anticipatory (2014).

Chapter 2

1. Wu (n.d.).
2. Gibson (1984).

Chapter 3

1. Rudder (2014).

Chapter 5

1. Ashton (1999).
2. Porter and Heppelman (2014).

Chapter 11

1. PSD2 regulation (n.d.).

Chapter 12

1. Home Depot Settlement (2014).
2. Sony Pictures Data Breach (2014).
3. Experian Hack (2020).
4. Talk Talk data breach (2015).
5. VTech Toys Hack (2015).
6. Cyber warfare leaves fingerprints (n.d.).

Chapter 13

1. Dubravac (2015).

Chapter 14

1. Slywotzky (1995).

Chapter 15

1. Metlife Wall Project (2013).

Chapter 17

1. Note that ripping (making digital copies of audio files from CDs) has been under legal scrutiny, and most countries will allow personal copies to be made, but sharing of these files is illegal in most places.

Chapter 19

1. Urban (2015).
2. Kelly (2016).
3. Kahneman (2013).

Chapter 20

1. Granovetter (1973).
2. Barabasi (2003).
3. Gladwell (2001).
4. Johnson (2013).

Chapter 21

1. Agile Manifesto (2001).
2. Syed (2019).

Chapter 22

1. Charan (2015).
2. Gates (1995).
3. Erickson (2012).

Chapter 24

1. NHS Funding Gap (n.d.).
2. NHS Funding Gap (n.d.).
3. Reminder services for healthcare (n.d.).
4. Waire Health (n.d.).
5. In the US, this could be up to 27 million by 2020. Companies such as MD Live are specialists in Telehealth and have been running for years, offering consultations that cover allergies, flu, or panic disorders, just to name a few.
6. Syncrophi (n.d.).
7. Deep Mind in the NHS (n.d.).

Chapter 25

1. IBM-eConsultancy Survey (2016).

Part 6

1. Pathadisha used for Metro passes (2020).

References

Agile Manifesto. n.d. http://agilemanifesto.org/.

Airbnb impact on rentals in France. n.d. https://journals.sagepub.com/doi/full/10.1177/0160017618821428.

Amazon patent for anticipatory shipment. n.d. https://techcrunch.com/2014/01/18/amazon-pre-ships/.

Ashton, K. n.d. https://en.wikipedia.org/wiki/Kevin_Ashton.

Asimov's 3 Laws of Robotics. n.d. https://en.wikipedia.org/wiki/Three_Laws_of_Robotics.

Asos Mobile Dominance. n.d. www.marketingweek.com/2016/10/18/asos-we-are-already-awesome-at-mobile-and-were-going-to-get-better/.

Autonomous car collision due to mistaking a truck for the sky. n.d. www.dezeen.com/2016/07/01/tesla-driver-killed-car-crash-news-driverless-car-autopilot/.

Barabasi, A.L. n.d. *Network Theory*. http://barabasi.com/networksciencebook/.

BBC Digital Media projet. n.d. www.bbc.co.uk/news/entertainment-arts-25925357.

BBC. n.d. *Fantasy Football Injury Leaks*. www.bbc.co.uk/news/newsbeat-56187365.

Blockchain for diamonds. n.d. www.wired.co.uk/article/blockchain-conflict-diamonds-everledger.

Boxtel, A. n.d. www.amandaboxtel.com/.

Brainprints. n.d. www.wired.co.uk/article/eeg-brainprint-biometric-identification.

Car sharing by Auto Majors. n.d. www.autoindustrylawblog.com/2016/11/21/more-auto-companies-bet-on-car-sharing/.

Charan, R. n.d. "The Attacker's Advantage."

Connected door bells. n.d. https://ring.com/.

Connecting AI to the brain. n.d. www.theverge.com/2017/3/27/15077864/elon-musk-neuralink-brain-computer-interface-ai-cyborgs.

Cukier, K. and V. Mayer-Schonberger. n.d. "Big Data: A Revolution That Will Transform How We Live, Work and Think."

Cyber warfare leaves fingerprints. n.d. www.ft.com/content/15e1acf0-0a47-11e6-b0f1-61f222853ff3.

Deep and Dark Web. n.d. Kaspersky Labs. www.kaspersky.com/resource-center/threats/deep-web.

Deep Mind in the NHS. n.d. www.newscientist.com/article/2113701-googles-deepmind-agrees-new-deal-to-share-nhs-patient-data/.

DeepMind helps Royal Free Hospital Trust, London, to predict Acute Kidney Infection. www.wired.co.uk/article/deepmind-nhs-ai-kidney-royal-free.

Design Value Index. n.d. www.dmi.org/?page=2015DVIandOTW.

Diem Association. n.d. www.diem.com/en-us/.

Dieter Rams design principles. n.d. https://en.wikipedia.org/wiki/Dieter_Rams.

Docker. n.d. *Containerisation.* www.docker.com/.

Dog control database. n.d. www.improvementservice.org.uk/news/august-2021/dog-control-database-proof-of-concept.

DOMO. n.d. https://web-assets.domo.com/blog/wp-content/uploads/2020/08/20-data-never-sleeps-8-final-01-Resize.jpg.

Dubravac, S. n.d. *Digital Destiny*, Chapter 8.

Dubravac, S. n.d. *Digital Destiny.* www.amazon.co.uk/Digital-Destiny-Data-Transform-Communicate/dp/1621573737.

Erickson, T. n.d. *How Mobile Technologies are Shaping a New Generation.* https://hbr.org/2012/04/the-mobile-re-generation.

Experian Hack. (n.d.). https://www.theguardian.com/business/2015/oct/01/experian-hack-t-mobile-credit-checks-personal-information

Flying a plane by thought. n.d. www.wired.com/2016/11/used-mind-fly-plane-around-seattle/.

Forbes. n.d. *Digital Transformation By Any Other Name.* www.forbes.com/forbes/welcome/?toURL=https://www.forbes.com/sites/jasonbloomberg/2014/07/31/digital-transformation-by-any-other-name/&refURL=&referrer=.

Frank Diana ecosystems. n.d. https://frankdiana.net/tag/ecosystems/.

Friedman, T. n.d. *Thank You For Being Late*, Chapter 2.

FT Innovate Conference. n.d. https://live.ft.com/SERIES/FT-INNOVATE-SERIES.

Gajar ka Halwa— an Indian carrot based dessert. https://en.wikipedia.org/wiki/Gajar_ka_halwa. The story was recounted to me by a certain Mr. Baskar V.

Galvani Bioelectronics. n.d. www.galvani.bio/

Gardner, H. and K. Davis. n.d. "The App Generation."

Gates, B. 1995. *Internet Memo 1995.* www.wired.com/2010/05/0526bill-gates-internet-memo/

Gibson, W. 1984. *The Neuromancer*, a 1984 Novel.

Gladwell, M. n.d. "The Tipping Point."

Global Sensors Numbers. n.d. https://globenewswire.com/news-release/2017/03/10/934261/0/en/Global-Sensors-in-Internet-of-Things-IoT-Devices-Market-2016-2022-100-billion-IoT-Connected-Devices-will-be-Installed-by-2025-to-Generate-Revenue-of-Close-to-10-Trillion.html.

Granovetter, M. n.d. *Strength of Weak Ties.* www.journals.uchicago.edu/doi/abs/10.1086/225469

Half the workforce are millennials. n.d. www.ft.com/content/30f03378-b46f-11e5-b147-e5e5bba42e51#axzz3xh6quN77.

Hall, E. n.d. *Philosophy.* www.youtube.com/watch?v=UzrOmf8sxkw.

Home Depot Settlement. n.d. https://threatpost.com/home-depot-agrees-to-19-5-million-settlement-to-end-2014-breach-nightmare/116884/.

Honda. n.d. *Designing Car Boots for the U.S.* www.strategy-business.com/article/07301?gko=5cd41.

House that Tweets. n.d. https://twitter.com/houseofcoates.

http://fortune.com/2017/02/02/vespa-piaggio-gita-robot/.

IBM-eConsultancy Survey. November 2016. "The New Marketing Reality."

In the US, this could be up to 27 million by 2020. Companies such as MD Live are specialists in Telehealth and have been running for years, offering consultations that cover allergies, flu, or panic disorders, just to name a few. https://welcome.mdlive.com/.

Interactive Design Foundation. n.d. *Adaptive vs Responsive Design.* www .interaction-design.org/literature/article/adaptive-vs-responsive-design.

Jeff Bezos's 2 pizza rule. n.d. www.businessinsider.com/jeff-bezos-two-pizza-rule-for-productive-meetings-2013-10?IR=T.

Johnson, S. n.d. "Where Good Ideas Come From." www.amazon.co.uk/dp/B0046ZRZ30/ref=dp-kindle-redirect?_encoding=UTF8&btkr=1.

Kahneman, D. n.d. *Thinking Fast & Slow.* www.amazon.co.uk/Thinking-Fast-Slow-Daniel-Kahneman/dp/0141033576.

KDS. n.d. www.kds.com/.

Kelly, K. n.d. "The Inevitable." www.amazon.co.uk/dp/B016JPTOUG/ref=dp-kindle-redirect?_encoding=UTF8&btkr=1.

Leinwand, P. February 2016. *Closing the Strategy-Execution Gap.* HBR. https://hbr.org/ideacast/2016/02/closing-the-strategy-execution-gap.

McKinsey Retail Analytics. n.d. www.mckinsey.com/business-functions/mckinsey-analytics/our-insights/how-to-win-in-the-age-of-analytics.

Meccano. n.d. https://en.wikipedia.org/wiki/Meccano.

Metlife Wall Project. n.d. "MongoDB." www.mongodb.com/customers/metlife.

MIT. n.d. *The Work of the Future—Building Better Jobs in an Age of Intelligent Machines.*

Mobile phones versus Toothbrushes. n.d. www.linkedin.com/pulse/really-more-mobile-phone-owners-than-toothbrush-jamie-turner/.

Music and age. n.d. www.classical-music.com/news/new-study-reveals-link-between-musical-taste-and-age.

Music and politics. n.d. https://thenextweb.com/insider/2012/07/12/republicans-have-less-diverse-music-taste-than-democrats-how-music-can-predict-our-political-leanings/#.tnw_eRl9Nfwl.

Music and socio-economics. n.d. www.sciencedaily.com/releases/2015/06/150603124545.htm

Neo4J Graph Databases. n.d. https://neo4j.com/.

NHS Funding Gap. n.d. https://fullfact.org/health/nhs-black-hole-size-funding-gap-2020/

Nuance. n.d. www.nuance.com/index.htm.

Nyquist Shannon Sampling Theorem. n.d. https://en.wikipedia.org/wiki/Nyquist%E2%80%93Shannon_sampling_theorem#Introduction.

Oxfam report. n.d. *8 Richest People.* www.oxfam.org.uk/media-center/press-releases/2017/01/eight-people-own-same-wealth-as-half-the-world.

Oxman, N. n.d. MIT. www.media.mit.edu/people/neri/overview/.

Pathadisha used for Metro passes. n.d. https://exametc.com/magazine/details.php?id=719.

Porter, M. and J. Heppelman in the Harvard Business Review. n.d. http://hbr.org/2014/11/how-smart-connected-products-are-transforming-competition/ar/pr.

Pranav Mistry 6th Sense. n.d. www.ted.com/talks/pranav_mistry_the_thrilling_potential_of_sixthsense_technology.

PSD2 regulation. n.d. www.paymentsuk.org.uk/policy/european-developments/payment-services-directive.

Quartz is an API. n.d. www.niemanlab.org/2015/05/quartz-is-an-api-the-path-ahead-for-the-business-site-thats-reshaping-digital-news/.

Reasons for transformation project failure. n.d. http://blogs.forrester.com/martin_gill/15-04-01-why_do_digital_business_transformations_fail; www.cmo.com/features/articles/2015/3/29/three-reasons-why-digital-transformation-projects-fail-.html#gs.xl_Nx_k; www.plusorminusseven.com/why-us/digital-transformational-projects-fail/.

Reimagining new customer onboarding with graph databases. n.d. https://neo4j.com/blog/telenor-neo4j-competitive-advantage-iam/.

Reminder services for healthcare. n.d. www.blipcare.com/.

Rent parking space. n.d. www.yourparkingspace.co.uk/?gclid=COe01KWX5tICFQw4Gwod_DEOXA

Ries, E. n.d. "The Lean Start Up."

Robertson, D with B. Breen. n.d. "'Brick By Brick' the Story of Lego Innovation."

Roomba intelligent vacuum cleaner. n.d. https://www.irobot.com/en_US/roomba.html

Rudder, C. n.d. "Dataclysm."

Sawhney, M. and D. Parekh. n.d. *Where Value Lives in a Networked World.* https://hbr.org/2001/01/where-value-lives-in-a-networked-world.

Slime mold and railway system. n.d. www.youtube.com/watch?v=GwKuFREOgmo.

Slime mold and maze. n.d. www.youtube.com/watch?v=F3z_mdaQ5ac.

Slywotzky, A. n.d. *Value Migration.* www.amazon.co.uk/Value-Migration-Competition-Management-Innovation/dp/0875846327.

Smart cameras. n.d. www.cnet.com/uk/pictures/connected-cameras-for-a-safer-smart-home-pictures/4/.

Smart lock. n.d. http://august.com/products/august-smart-lock/.

Smart refrigerators. n.d. http://uk.businessinsider.com/the-complete-history-of-internet-fridges-and-connected-refrigerators-2016-1.

Social selling. n.d. *Avon millionaire.* www.bbc.co.uk/news/uk-england-wear-11089927

Sony Pictures Data Breach. (n.d.). www.vanityfair.com/hollywood/2015/02/sony-hacking-seth-rogen-evan-goldberg.

Splunk. n.d. www.splunk.com/en_us/software/splunk-enterprise.html

Starlings communicate with 7 closest neighbours. n.d. http://journals.plos.org/ploscompbiol/article?id=10.1371/journal.pcbi.1002894.

Stuxnet. n.d. https://en.wikipedia.org/wiki/Stuxnet.

Syed, M. n.d. "Black Box Thinking."

Syncrophi. n.d. www.syncrophi.com/.

Talk Talk data breach. n.d. www.independent.co.uk/news/business/news/talktalk-fine-data-breach-theft-customers-information-stolen-record-penalty-a7346316.html.

TCS Clever Energy. n.d. www.tcs.com/tcs-launches-iot-powered-clever-energy-solution-to-help-enterprises-accelerate-shift-towards-net-zero-emission.

The Economist. n.d. *World Population to Peak at 9.7bn in 2064.* www.economist.com/graphic-detail/2020/07/17/a-new-forecast-says-the-worlds-population-will-peak-at-97bn-in-2064.

T-mobile. n.d. www.telekom.com/en/company/management-unplugged/francois-fleutiaux/details/vehicle-data-is-more-profitable-than-the-car-itself-516208.

Tor. n.d. Anonymous web. https://en.wikipedia.org/wiki/Tor_(anonymity_network).

TPBank foiled heist. n.d. www.theguardian.com/technology/2016/may/16/vietnamese-bank-foils-1m-cyber-heist.

Two thirds of digital projects fail. n.d. www.consultancy.uk/news/2656/two-thirds-of-digital-transformation-projects-fail.

Urban, T. n.d. "Wait But Why 'The AI Revolution: The Road to Superintelligence'." http://waitbutwhy.com/2015/01/artificial-intelligence-revolution-1.html.

Velux Windows. n.d. www.velux.co.uk/.

VTech Toys Hack. n.d. https://www.theguardian.com/technology/2015/nov/30/vtech-toys-hack-private-data-parents-children

VUCA. n.d. https://en.wikipedia.org/wiki/Volatility,_uncertainty,_complexity_and_ambiguity.

Waire Health. n.d. www.waire.health/.

Wired Magazine. n.d. *Tesla Over The Air Updates.* www.wired.com/insights/2014/02/teslas-air-fix-best-example-yet-internet-things/.

Wu, T. n.d. *The Master Switch—The Rise and Fall of Information Empires.*

Zara and Next Versus Asos and BooHoo. n.d. https://qz.com/951055/a-new-generation-of-even-faster-fashion-is-leaving-hm-and-zara-in-the-dust/.

Suggested Reference Books

Azhar, A. 2021. *Exponential*. Cornerstone Digital.

Barabasi, A.L. 2014. *Linked*. Basic Books.

Boxtrom, N. 2016. *Superintelligence: Paths, Dangers, Strategies*. Oxford University Press.

Bradly, A.J. and M.P. McDonald. 2011. *The Social Organization*. Harvard Business Review Press.

Breen, B. and D. Robertson. 2013. *Brick by Brick*. Cornerstone Digital.

Brett, K. 2012. *Bank 3.0*. Marshall Cavendish Business.

Charan, R. 2015. *Attackers Advantage*. PublicAffairs.

Cukier, K. and V.M. Schonberger. 2013. *Big Data: A Revolution That Will Transform How We Live, Work and Think*. John Murray.

Dubravac, S. 2015. *Digital Destiny*. Regnery Publishing.

Epstein, D. 2019. *Range*. Macmillan.

Frank, M., B. Pring, and P. Roehrig. 2014. *Code Halos*. John Wiley & Sons.

Gada, K. 2021. *ATOM*. Business Express Press.

Harford, T. 2016. *Messy*. Little, Brown Book Group.

Ismail, S. 2014. *Exponential Organisations*. Diversion Books.

Johnson, S. 2010. *Where Good Ideas Come From*. Penguin.

Kahnemann, D. 2012. *Thinking Fast & Slow*. Penguin.

Kelly, K. 2016. *Inevitable*. Viking Publishing.

Knapp, J., J. Zeratski, and B. Kowitz. 2016. *Sprint*. Transworld Digital.

Marcus, G. and E. Davis. 2019. *Rebooting AI*. Pantheon Books.

Negroponte, N. and A.A. Knopf. 1995. *Being Digital*.

Nielssen, L. and N. Burlingame. 2013. *A Simple Introduction to Data Science*. New Street Communications.

Olson, P. 2013. *We Are Anonymous*. Cornerstone Digital.

Rao, V. 2018. *Breaking Smart*. Ribbonfarm.com.

Raskino, R. and G. Waller. 2015. *Digital To The Core*. Routledge.

Rauser, A. n.d. *Digital Strategy*. Self-published, Amazon Kindle.

Ries, E. 2011. *Lean Start Up*. Porfolio Penguin.

Rudder, C. 2014. *Dataclysm*. Crown.

Saldanha, T. 2019. *Why Digital Transformations Fail*. Berrett-Koehler Publishers.

Schadler, T., J. Bernoff, and J. Ask. 2014. *Mobile Mind Shift*. Groundswell Press.

Schmidt , E. and J. Cohen. 2013. *The New Digital Age*. John Murray.

Schwab, K. 2017. *The Fourth Industrial Revolution*. Penguin.

Scoble, R. and S. Israel. 2014. *Age of Context*. Patrick Brewster Press.

Siebel, T. 2019. *Digital Transformation in the Age of Extinction*. Rosetta Books.

Stickdorn, M. and J. Schneider. (Ed). 2012. *This is Service Design Thinking*. BIS Publishers.

Syed, M. 2015. *Black Box Thinking*. John Murray.

Thiel, P. 2014. *Zero To One*. Virgin Digital.

Tunguz, T. and F. Bien. 2016. *Winning With Data*. John Wiley & Sons.

About the Author

Ved Sen has been working on emerging technologies from the mid-1990s. Starting with the Internet and ecommerce, and going on to interactive television, mobile apps, the Internet of things, augmented reality, and AI, he has been at the coal face of driving projects that use new technologies to make a difference in organizations. Ved currently works as a Digital Evangelist and Innovation Lead for Tata Consultancy Services, in London, and his day job involves solving problems that don't have ready solutions.

Ved completed his Graduation in Economics at Presidency College, Kolkata, and went to the Indian Institute of Management, Ahmedabad, one of India's best business schools. But he was never drawn to mainstream career options, and spent time in advertising and journalism before discovering the world of Internet and technology. Thanks to his educational background, he has always evaluated technology from the logical perspective of a lay person and tried to ask and answer fundamental questions about the structure, use, and value of technologies.

A self-confessed techno-optimist, Ved believes that technology can be used to solve some of the world's bigger problems, but that it also influences society, culture, politics, and every other aspect of our lives. His current work and thinking also focuses on using technology for driving social value as well as business outcomes.

Ved grew up in Kolkata, India, and spent time in Bangalore, the tech hub of India, before settling in London where he has been for much of the past 20 years. He now lives in St. Albans, on the outskirts of London with his wife and daughter. He plays soccer and badminton on weekends and practices on his saxophone in his nonexistent spare time.

Index

OTHER TITLES IN THE COLLABORATIVE INTELLIGENCE COLLECTION

Jim Spohrer and Haluk Demirkan, Editors

- *How Organizations Can Make the Most of Online Learning* by David Guralnick
- *Business and Emerging Technologies* by George Baffour
- *Teaching Higher Education to Lead* by Sam Choon-Yin
- *How to Talk to Data Scientists* by Jeremy Elser
- *Leadership in The Digital Age* by Niklas Hageback
- *Cultural Science* by William Sims Bainbridge
- *The Future of Work* by Yassi Moghaddam, Heather Yurko, and Haluk Demirkan
- *Advancing Talent Development* by Philip Gardner and Heather N. Maietta
- *Virtual Local Manufacturing Communities* by William Sims Bainbridge
- *T-Shaped Professionals* by Yassi Moghaddam, Haluk Demirkan, and James Spohrer
- *The Interconnected Individual* by Hunter Hastings and Jeff Saperstein

Concise and Applied Business Books

The Collection listed above is one of 30 business subject collections that Business Expert Press has grown to make BEP a premiere publisher of print and digital books. Our concise and applied books are for…

- Professionals and Practitioners
- Faculty who adopt our books for courses
- Librarians who know that BEP's Digital Libraries are a unique way to offer students ebooks to download, not restricted with any digital rights management
- Executive Training Course Leaders
- Business Seminar Organizers

Business Expert Press books are for anyone who needs to dig deeper on business ideas, goals, and solutions to everyday problems. Whether one print book, one ebook, or buying a digital library of 110 ebooks, we remain the affordable and smart way to be business smart. For more information, please visit www.businessexpertpress.com, or contact sales@businessexpertpress.com.

www.ingramcontent.com/pod-product-compliance
Lightning Source LLC
Chambersburg PA
CBHW061147220326
41599CB00025B/4380